UNDERST

SASSIE II

A SECOND NOVEL OF DOG AND HUMAN COMMUNICATION

HELEN A. BEMIS

outskirts
press

Understanding Sassie II
A Second Novel of Dog and Human Communication
All Rights Reserved.
Copyright © 2019 Helen A. Bemis
v3.0

This is a work of fiction. Names, characters, businesses, places, events, locales, and incidents are either the products of the author's imagination or used in a fictitious manner. Any resemblance to actual persons, living or dead, or actual events is purely coincidental.

The opinions expressed in this manuscript are solely the opinions of the author and do not represent the opinions or thoughts of the publisher. The author has represented and warranted full ownership and/or legal right to publish all the materials in this book.

This book may not be reproduced, transmitted, or stored in whole or in part by any means, including graphic, electronic, or mechanical without the express written consent of the publisher except in the case of brief quotations embodied in critical articles and reviews.

Outskirts Press, Inc.
http://www.outskirtspress.com

ISBN: 978-1-9772-1066-1

Cover image by Mechelle Roskiewicz

Outskirts Press and the "OP" logo are trademarks belonging to Outskirts Press, Inc.

PRINTED IN THE UNITED STATES OF AMERICA

Praise for *Understanding Sassie*
and for *Understanding Sassie II*

I so enjoyed returning to the characters I first met in *Understanding Sassie.* I like reading a continuing story about familiar characters while being introduced to new information. *Sassie II* does both. The widening circle of people and animals that are inter-related help carry the narrative through plausible problems. This story demonstrates how the human family/ community works together to solve problems, while giving new insights into how animals work together to help each other as well. I'm thrilled to know a third book is forthcoming. The building of this peaceful place reminds me of Jan Karon's "Mitford" series. I look forward to learning where Sassy takes me and what Sassy has to teach me next!

Jane Stratton, Registered Nurse.

Understanding Sassie II is a wonderful and heartwarming story that brings about lots of different emotions. While reading about the lives of the various characters and their connections with each other and with the dogs in the book, I found it to be suspenseful, happy, sad, fun, and an especially great love story. Enjoyed it immensely!

Nancy Pic, Dental Hygienist.

What a delight to read Helen's second book of her series, "Understanding Sassie." It was exciting to fellow her characters that I have grown to love. Helen's writes with such detail that I feel I can smell the coffee brewing at the animal shelter. Through Helen's words and work I have come to appreciate how intuitive, intelligent, and loyal dogs can be. If you love dogs as I do, you'll appreciate *Understanding Sassie II*. Thank you, Helen, for a good read.

Judy Rosebrook, Retired nurse, singer

CONTENTS

Dedication i
Acknowledgments iii
Preface v

1. Peg and Patrick 1
2. The Dog Thief 8
3. Champ 12
4. Millie 17
5. Donald's and Ruth's Concerns 22
6. Puppy Play Day 30
7. Psych 38
8. Donald, Ruth, and the Farm 43
9. Donald, Ruth, and the Cat 48
10. Jane, Millie, and Ruth 54
11. The Library 59
12. A Bath and a Hurricane 62
13. Reading to Sassie 66
14. Sharon and Sassie 71

15.	Gulf Coast Evacuation	75
16.	Psych's Dog Foster Home	81
17.	Ruth's and Jim's Saturdays	84
18.	Ruth, Millie, and Puppy Socialization Class	87
19.	Mike and Millie	90
20.	Ruth and Her CPDT Test Preparations	93
21.	Planning Something Special	96
22.	Puppy Socialization Class	99
23.	Miniature Golf	103
24.	Ruth's Accident	106
25.	A Teddy Bear in Class	110
26.	Ruth Goes Home	115
27.	Sassie Concerns	118
28.	Sharon Explains	121

Cast of Characters	127
Glossary/Vocabulary	129
About the Author	131
About the Artist	133
Review This Book?	135

DEDICATION

To all those who show kindness and compassion.

ACKNOWLEDGMENTS

To my beloved husband, Bruce: A special "thank you" to you for your patience, encouragement, and understanding during the writing of this book

To Doug Cooper: You may hold the title of coach, but you have become so much more. You're my teacher, my punctuation specialist, and a special friend. I've often said that you are worth your weight in gold. Actually, you are worth more than that to me. Your wisdom and "fine tuning" of my writing has been, for me, invaluable!

To Mechelle: Thank you for sharing your art. My covers are special because of your talent in drawing awesome dogs. It is an honor to be able to use these pictures.

To you, the reader: Thank you for accepting Sassie as your language-of-dogs' teacher and for your recognition of how love and respect when used in dog training will always conquer fear.

PREFACE

"Grandma, what is going to happen to the characters in *Understanding Sassie?*" Jacob asked. My grandson had enjoyed reading my book but wanted to know more about its characters. He continued his questioning and asked, "Are you going to write more about Sassie and all the other people in the book?" I found validation in his excitement about my book. Teaching by using a story has always been, for me, an effective way to help someone remember an important lesson.

In my many years of teaching dog obedience, I have discovered that not all humans understand what the dog is trying to tell them. Although I've enjoyed my opportunities to teach classes on dog communication (the body language of dogs), my goal has always been to reach a wider audience.

I believe if you can understand what someone is saying, any fear or confusion can be eliminated. We can listen to them and feel comfortable in recognizing what they are saying to us.

I also believe that if fear and confusion are eliminated, we are more inclined to listen and respect someone's (or some dog's) communication.

My grandson was not the only one to urge me to write more about Sassie and her friends. I'm grateful for so many others that have encouraged me.

If you are reading this book and have not read *Understanding Sassie*, there is no need to read *Understanding Sassie* before reading this second book. I have given enough information that you can read the two books in any order.

I invite you to enjoy *Understanding Sassie II,* as it shares more lessons, stories, and adventures.

Helen

1

PEG AND PATRICK

Peg's mom had only stared at the puppy in disbelief. She was proud of the fact that she kept her house spotless. The neighbors all said that if an award was given for the cleanest home, Peg's mom would be the neighborhood winner.

Seeing this dirty, long-haired dog, Peg's mom began screaming, "No! That puppy will not come into this house!" Peg had pulled Lady closer to her chest as her mom continued to yell. "That filthy animal needs to go!"

Peg could feel that Lady was shivering. "Stop yelling! You are scaring Lady!" Peg's tears started to flow. She began to step backwards.

Peg's father had just come home, and when he heard the shouting, he walked around the house to see what it was about. Seeing Peg crying, he asked his wife, "Honey, why are you yelling at Peg?"

He put his arm around Peg, and then he noticed

the puppy. He gently took Lady into his arms, "What a beautiful puppy!"

His wife lowered her voice but was determined to get rid of this bundle of dirt. With her hands on her hips, she announced to her husband, "We are not going to keep this mutt!"

Peg and Patrick were enjoying their daily walk. This was a routine the teenagers often shared, and today was no exception. Only today, they were also walking their young dogs.

It was a sunny spring day; the temperature was comfortable, and the soft breeze was just enough to tickle the leaves. When they got to Riverview Park, they decided to sit on one of the benches there. Patrick reached down to unclip the leash from the collar of his dog, Pal. Peg had already unclipped her leash from Lady's collar.

The teenagers smiled as the dogs gave their play bows and danced off to play a game of chase. "I never tire of watching them play. Remember the first time we saw the play bow?" Patrick asked Peg. "With their butts in the air and their front legs and elbows on the ground, it really did look like they were doing bows."

Peg replied, "Can you believe it has been six months since we found these two puppies?"

Understanding Sassie II

"Remember how interested they were in our picnic food?" Patrick replied with a smile.

"I was surprised at their willingness to trust us."

Patrick continued, "Peg, you knew they were hungry, and your idea of giving them a trail of treats was brilliant!"

Peg looked at Lady chasing Pal and said, "Yes, that was easy, compared to your dad's and my mom's unwillingness to accept our dogs. I can still remember how horrified my mom became when I brought Lady home."

Although she had told Patrick her story many times, she began to tell the story again:

"Lady was in my arms. When I saw Mom, I announced, 'Guess what! This is Lady, my new puppy!'"

That was when my mom began screaming that I could not keep my puppy. I was in love with Lady, and I was determined to beg, if I needed to, for keeping my dog. "I will give her a bath. I'll take care of Lady, and you can use all my allowance for any food or other things she may need."

Peg's father looked down at the puppy. He had already fallen in love with Lady. "Honey, we could keep her for a month and see how she fits into our lifestyle. She might be an excellent security system when she gets older. Can't you at least agree to a trial period?"

His wife slowly responded, 'I will let that dog stay for now, but Peg, you and your father are responsible for all the work, care, and expenses of this dog. I do not want anything to do with this puppy!"

"Yes," said Patrick. "At that time, I thought I, too, was going to have a big problem with both of my parents. I believed that they would not want me to have a puppy! I remember walking slowly home. I planned to enter the house quietly and hide Pal upstairs in my bedroom."

"Your mom surprised you," Peg interjected.

"Yes, my mom had just turned off the television when I walked in. Her reaction surprised me. My mom's eyes seemed to light up and she said, 'What an adorable puppy! Can I hold him? Does he have a name?'"

Patrick had reluctantly handed the puppy to his mom and told her, "His name is Pal."

Patrick's mom instantly fell in love with Pal. "He not only looks a lot like the dog I had as a child, but you gave this puppy the same name as my childhood dog." Patrick's mom said this softly while she caressed Pal's fur. Then she gently placed him on the floor and watched Pal begin to sniff around the room.

Patrick's father would be coming home soon. Concerned about his father's reaction to Pal, Patrick had looked at his mom and asked, "Do you think Dad will let me keep him?"

Before she could answer, his father walked in the door. He stopped, stared at the puppy, and then loudly questioned, "Why is this mutt in our house?"

The very loud voice made Pal act small. It was a submissive posture. Pal was trying to tell this loud person that he would not be a problem. As Patrick's father continued to yell, Pal did a submissive pee to try, once again, in a different way, to prove he really was no threat to anyone. "He is peeing in the house! Take him outside, now!" Patrick's father had continued to yell, and he had pointed at the door. Patrick grabbed Pal and ran out that door.

His mother saw the look on Patrick's face and made a firm decision. She was going to keep this dog. "What is your problem? Bad day at work? Traffic tie-up? You can stop the noise right now and listen to me. Do you love hunting?"

"Yes," her husband had replied.

"And have you said many times that you wanted a good and reliable alarm system?"

"Yes," her husband said again.

Patrick's mom pointed her finger at her husband and in an authoritative voice said, "Let me tell you why this dog is going to stay. First: if this dog is trained properly, he could grow up to be a good hunting companion. Second: dogs have a keen sense of smell and hearing. They can alert us to smoke and fire long before any smoke alarm would tell us. The security of a dog protecting his home is far better than any noisy alarm and faster than a call to the police. Pal will be cared for by Patrick and me, so you will accept Pal as the newest member of our home!"

Reluctantly, Patrick's father had said, "I will accept this dog a lot easier when he learns some house manners."

When Patrick returned with Pal, he began to say, "I'll give up my...," but his father stopped him in mid-sentence.

"No need to say anything, son, your mom has explained all, and Pal will be living here."

The teenagers were quiet for a while and Patrick softly said, "I don't think these puppies would have survived the weather last winter if we had not rescued them when we did. Remember how the temperatures got to 40 below zero, and how there were yardstick-deep snow drifts around the area?"

Peg agreed and added, "Remember the night you were able to have Pal sleep in bed with you?"

"Yes," Patrick responded, "You said that's also when you were able to have Lady lie on your bed."

Peg smiled and remarked, "The puppies were like little heaters that kept us nice and warm."

Patrick started to smile and said, "I've got a new dog joke. Do you want to hear it?"

Peg nodded yes, and Patrick began, "A Great Dane and a Golden Retriever were walking down a path when the Dane confided to the Golden, 'My life is a mess. My human is mean, and I'm as nervous as a hamster.'

"'Why don't you go see a psychiatrist?' suggested the Golden.

"'I can't,' replied the Dane, 'I'm not allowed on the couch.'"

Peg began to laugh, and when Patrick looked at the puppies, he started to laugh as well, "Take a look at those silly puppies. Not only are they having fun, but I always seem to laugh when I watch them. One of my favorite games to watch them play is the stallion game,"

Peg commented, "That is a good description of that type of play, because they look like two horses fighting. They rise up onto their back paws with the front legs in the air, waving their paws at one another."

Patrick added, "They maneuver with their back legs and try to get into position for a good fighting stance."

Peg began to reflect on how much they had discovered about the dogs' language. She said, "That is why I like to go to the Puppy Play Days at the Riverview Shelter. Miss Millie explains what the dogs are saying to each other. Like how to know the difference between real play and real fighting. She says the key is the play bow given before the play fight. The play bow says that whatever the puppies do after the bow is not real fighting but just playing."

Pat remarked, "Sometimes it does sound like a real fight, but the dogs understand their dog language."

Peg added, "I'm glad Miss Millie helps us understand their dog talk. That reminds me, we don't want to forget that there is a puppy play date this Saturday."

2

THE DOG THIEF

He had always loved money. He loved what it bought. He loved the power it gave him. He also enjoyed how money made him feel. To him, money was not only important, but he believed that getting money was his mission in life.

His name was George, but they called him "Psych." It was not because he could read someone's mind but because he could predict a person's actions, and when it came to dog-fighting, he had an instinct that seemed spooky. He especially understood anything that had to do with the business of dog-fighting and the people who loved to see them fight. He admired the winners of a dog-fight. He loved the anticipation of a dog-fight and the rush of emotion during the battle. Seeing his dog win never stopped being a peak moment.

He knew how to breed fighting dogs because he had been breeding them for most of his life. He

Understanding Sassie II

would match his most vicious bitch to a muscular and strong-minded stud. He'd kept the most aggressive pup and sold the rest of the litter for a good price. He had learned how important it was to remove the puppies from their mom as soon as they were born. If he did not remove the puppies quick enough, the mother's temperament would destroy all the puppies in the litter.

Psych had developed the power of anger to instill fear. He wondered if this was at the time that he had overheard his mom talking to a friend about her fear of anger.

She had said, "It was an incident that happened when I was eight years old. My father had been out in the driveway screaming at my brother. Stomping into the house, my father grabbed his hunting rifle, loaded it, and then mumbled something about teaching my brother a lesson. He slammed the door on his way out and began to point the rifle at my brother.

"I was able to see the two of them as I looked out the window. My brother suddenly grabbed the end of the rifle. They struggled. The gun shot was loud and sudden. I began to sob. I was too afraid to continue to look at this fearful scene. It was a welcome relief when I discovered that no one had been hurt, but I never forgot the fear I felt at this time of uncontrolled anger."

Psych smiled and thought again about the wisdom he had gained from his life experiences. *I*

*remember the time I had read an article about elec-
tronic shock collars. It was written by a well-respect-
ed organization. It had advised the non-use of the
collar for training because it could cause aggression
in the dog.*

*That was a helpful bit of advice for me because
I wanted aggression in my fighting dogs. It did help
me with my dog-fighting training.*

He had done this dog-fighting work for years,
until the government raided his illegal dog-fighting
pit. It was just pure luck that he was not at his place
when they made the raid. He was out of town and
using his stud for a large-purse competition. The
only reason he brought the bitch along was for a
chance at breeding her to another top fighting stud.

He lost much of his assets in that raid but managed to flee the state before the authorities could
catch him. "It's a good thing that I had kept part of
my money in some out-of-state banks," he had remarked at that time.

"A while back I found me the perfect location," he had boasted. He remembered, *I'd been
working on this 50-acre run-down farm. When
the farmer's doctor told the farmer that he had
terminal cancer, that was when he began to rely
entirely on my help.*

*I found it easy to trick the owner into signing over
his deed to the farm. The farmer had been taking a
lot of medications and did not realize what he was
signing. He had no need for a farm when he would*

soon be heading into the hospital. Psych claimed, "I did him a favor!"

At that time, he had been stealing the smaller unsupervised dogs from the Riverview area. Sometimes he was able to capture a few from the local dog park. It was easy to do when the small dog was friendly, and the owner was paying little or no attention to their dog.

Psych also discovered a few area neighborhood yards where the dog owners paid little or no attention to their dogs. Whenever the owners would release their small dog into the outdoor yard, Psych would watch the actions of the owners. If they ignored the barking of their dogs and seemed to be unconcerned about giving their canine any attention, he knew he would have a successful grab and go.

It seemed easy to stuff the little animal into his pocket or bag and disappear.

3

CHAMP

Psych had been quietly working on building an awesome dog-fighting area. He insulated the inside of a huge barn on the farm and covered the windows with pull-down black-out shades. Every inch of the barn was completely renovated.

During this time, he began to train a new group of dogs. The bait dogs he had already stolen had been a good and successful training tool. Slowly, as he traveled the dog-fighting circuit, his stud, Champ, had successfully won a large amount of cash.

He decided that it was time to open his own fighting location; the barn was to become his fighting "crown jewel."

I wonder what to use as a draw that won't alert the cops? He needed to be careful and only get the right dog-fighting people. *I could set up a good-sized purse. Should I call this a "Grand Opening" of this location?*

He decided not to enter Champ into this "Grand Opening" fight; instead, he'd use this to check out the competition. Yep, Champ had been his best fighter. No need to let the locals know just how good Champ could be.

Champ knew he was unbeatable. His undefeated fighting record proved this fact. Champ's body was a roadmap of scars, his coat of honor. Champ no longer had two intact ears. One ear was more of a half ear, and the other had been completely bitten off. *Losing that ear was better than losing the fight,* he thought. *That bulldog was one mean canine. I almost lost that fight! Lucky for me I was meaner.*

Champ loved to see his opponent act small. (Psych called it "being submissive.") This dog might lift his paw and do a lip flick. Other appeasing gestures and calming signals might be used to say, "I mean you no harm." Champ knew that when this opponent realized that these signals were being ignored, he would need to fight for his life. This could make him a dangerous opponent.

If Champ hesitated when he saw the calming signals, knowing that the other dog did not wish to fight, Psych would punish Champ with an electrical shock through the collar. This painful shock would urge Champ to attack the other dog. Champ recognized that this was the only way to stop the shooting pain.

Champ knew the body language of a fighter. Anyone that understood dog body language also knew that Champ was always ready for a fight. He would be leaning forward with his eyes staring at his opponent, tail up and slightly waving, displaying his excitement and determination to defeat his competition. Champ's hair stuck up along his back. His lips were drawn into a taught lip position that exposed many of his teeth. He emitted a growl that sounded threatening and indicated that Champ meant business, and this was true; his business was to win the fight.

Champ had always spent a fair amount of time in his crate. Even so, he did not lack for exercise nor good food. Psych made sure Champ's muscles were always ready for fighting, and Champ's meals were always the top grades of meat. The only time he was the least bit hungry was just before a fight. Psych believed it was best if Champ wanted to eat his opponent.

However, Champ never felt a loving hand, nor did he know any other lifestyle. He did fear Psych and his use of the electronic shock collar. It was a painful tool Psych liked to use as punishment.

The large barn where Champ lived was located a great distance from the Riverview Village. The house and barn were in the middle of a 50-acre, rundown farm. Various weeds became the field "crops," and young trees and bushes randomly dotted the area. The house needed paint.

Although flowers had originally been planted around the house, only wild lilies and milkweeds remained. Crab grass made up much of what was once a front lawn. The only majestic growth was the huge maple tree that stood at the corner of a dandelion-infested driveway.

Psych was happy with the overall look of the place. The run-down house seemed to look like it was saying, "Stay away," and the half-fallen chain-link fence added to the go-away ambiance.

When he gave directions to driving to his dog fights, they were simple: "You just need to head south on Route 714 until you reach a covered bridge. As soon as you cross the bridge, turn right. Travel on this road until you see a large red boulder. Turn here. Continue driving. When you see a large sign on a maple tree that says, 'Smile,' turn into this driveway. Follow the driveway around to the back of the house. You should park in the area near the barn. That way your vehicle will not be seen from the dirt road."

Psych's barn was made to be completely soundproof. Even the doors that were at the entrance to the barn were soundproofed.

The farm was located on the county line; Psych knew that the local sheriff never bothered to travel out to this area,

Psych was pleased that the many trees and bushes along the roads heading to the farm created the illusion of wilderness.

Psych boasted, "I've succeeded in creating the perfect invisible dog-fight location."

Today, Psych had made his usual run into Riverview to buy some top-quality meat for his dogs. He parked his ten-year-old Ford pickup just in front of the village butcher. He noticed a fancy sign in front of a nearby store that read, "Riverview Animal Shelter. Want that special dog or cat? We have many good animals available for adoption. We're open from 10 a.m. until 4 p.m. weekdays and on Saturday by appointment only. Take a flyer to learn more details." The flyers sat on a table underneath the sign.

Psych went over to the table, took a flyer and began to read, "No need to fill out an application for adoption. You can stop by, select your animal and take him home that same day."

Psych thought, *Wow, that's interesting! Maybe I should give a look-see at this shelter. If there are no applications, I might be able to get my supply of bait animals there. That would make it nice and easy for me. Think I may go over there sometime soon.*

4

MILLIE

Millie was singing as she loaded the breakfast dishes into the dishwasher, a morning chore she enjoyed. She believed it might have something to do with the fact that she was now Mike's wife.

As she looked down at Goldie, lying by her feet, she acknowledged that this dog had been the gentle and wise teacher that taught both Mike and her the true meaning of love. It had been Mike who had named this dog "Goldie." He had felt that it would be a fitting name for her from the first time he saw this golden-haired dog. They both suspected that Goldie had some Golden Retriever in her bloodline.

Millie smiled as she thought back to the day of their marriage. Mike was the one who suggested that they have the wedding and the reception at the large Riverview Park. Because they were both residents of the Riverview Community, they were allowed to reserve a large area of this park at no cost. They were able to use several pavilions; the tennis court, which could be used as a doggy play area; and a beautiful garden near the water. It was the perfect location. Millie had worried about the possibility of rain, but she was happy that Mike's sunshine prediction proved accurate.

A sudden movement brought Millie's attention to the window over the sink. Moving along the window sill was a beautiful butterfly. Behind the butterfly could be seen an emerald green lawn and islands of "flutter-by" flowers. The first time she told Mike that she would plant "flutter-by" flowers only, he looked puzzled. "I've never heard of that type of flower," he commented.

She explained, "'Flutter-by' is my secret name for the most beautiful of butterflies." Mike also discovered that Millie considered the milkweed a "flutter-by" flower.

"The milkweeds' leaves are important to the life of the Monarch 'flutter-by,'" Millie explained. "They will lay their eggs on the milkweed leaves. When the eggs hatch, the babies feed on those milkweed leaves."

At Goldie's yip, Millie turned and saw that Mike had entered the kitchen. "Have you seen my Animal Control baseball cap?" Mike asked.

Millie thought for a minute and replied, "I believe I saw it on the stand in the bedroom." Mike was dressed for his job at the Animal Control Office but

Understanding Sassie II

still needed his cap. "Mike," Millie asked, "What are your plans for today?"

Mike replied, "I'm not sure. I will be making a stop at the Riverview Animal Shelter and talk to Jane, Ruth, and Donald." Jane was the shelter's supervisor, and Ruth and Donald were volunteers who usually helped Jane.

"I've been told that Sassie will be there today. Do you think Goldie would like to come with me and play with her?"

Sassie was a Golden-Retriever mix adopted by Ruth. Sassie was Goldie's daughter, but only Sassie and Goldie knew this.

At the mention of Sassie's name, Goldie's ears came up and were pointed toward Mike.

Goldie loved to play with Sassie and realized that Mike was saying something about bringing her to see Sassie. She started to get up and let them know that she did want to see Sassie.

"Yes," Millie answered, "Take Goldie with you. You can see that she is already doing her happy dance. I told you she understands everything we say."

Mike laughed and quickly retrieved his cap from the bedroom. When he returned, he saw Goldie blocking the doorway. It was almost as if she said, "I will not let you leave without me!"

It was true, Goldie had decided to block the door and was indeed saying, "Take me with you." Her tail was wagging and her whole body was moving with excitement.

Mike grabbed one of Millie's breakfast muffins and took a big bite. Then he gave Millie a crumb-filled good-bye kiss. He thought it would make Millie laugh...and she did.

He grabbed Goldie's leash, quickly clipped it to Goldie's collar, and out the door they went.

Millie started the dishwasher, then picked up the morning paper. She sat on a chair by the kitchen table and relaxed. Her second cup of coffee was already on the table.

Slowly scanning each section of the newspaper, she stopped when she saw a small headline that read, "Why are so many dogs disappearing?" She began to study the article. She thought, *the article seems to be suggesting that there might be a dog thief in the area*.

The thought reminded her of something that she had noticed at her wedding. Thinking back to the activity around the dog play area, she remembered seeing a stranger acting a little too interested in the dogs playing there: *At the time, I told myself there was no reason to be concerned, because the park was a public area. This news article makes me wonder if I had been looking at a dog thief. I wonder why anyone would want to steal a dog?*

Looking for a reason to call the Riverview Animal Shelter and talk to Ruth about the newspaper article, she remembered that Ruth had suggested to her the possibility of doing dog-training classes.

Ruth said that this could be a way to help supplement the shelter's income.

Understanding Sassie II

She folded the newspaper and decided to call the shelter.

Jane sounded happy when she answered the phone, "Hi, Millie. Glad you called. Donald and I were just talking about the funny things that the puppies do during Puppy Play Time. This Saturday will be Puppy Play Time, and we wondered if you would like to bring Goldie with you?"

Millie thought for a minute, then said, "That might be a good idea. Goldie would be a good older dog that would show the puppies proper dog manners. Yes, I think I will bring her on Saturday."

"May I speak to Ruth? She had suggested some ideas for dog classes, and I'd like to talk to her about it."

5

DONALD'S AND RUTH'S CONCERNS

Sassie had become Valerie's Diabetic Alert Dog and as such became a constant companion and comfort to her. Valerie was Ruth's mom; Ruth enjoyed seeing the loving relationship between Sassie and her mom.

Lately, Valerie seemed to be tripping and falling down a lot. She appeared to be weak and confused as well. The doctor had scheduled several tests for Valerie to be done today at the local hospital.

Ruth decided to bring Sassie to the shelter rather than leaving her at home alone. It was a good plan because Sassie enjoyed being a greeter at the shelter. Sassie also liked to go into every area and visit all the residents. Her visits seemed to have a calming effect on everyone she visited, animals and humans alike.

Sassie never stared into a resident's eyes and often gave a play bow to show her willingness to play.

Sometimes she would sniff or yawn to try to calm the nervous resident.

As Ruth entered the shelter, she saw Donald. Donald got down on his knees, and Sassie ran to give Donald a kiss.

"How's my favorite girl?"

Donald was talking to Sassie, but Ruth replied, "I'm fine. Thank you for asking."

Donald made a face at Ruth and then stood up. He wanted to ask Ruth a question about Valerie. Ruth and Donald had discovered, last year, that they both had the same mother, Valerie. Donald had become fond of his birth mother, and Ruth enjoyed having the big brother she never had before.

"How long is Valerie going to be at the Hospital for her tests?" Donald asked Ruth.

"I'm not sure," she answered, "but the doctor said the testing would take most of the day. The doctor did promise to call me later this afternoon."

Just then Mike entered the lobby. Goldie started to do her happy dance and kept pulling her leash to greet Sassie.

"Easy, easy, we'll let you play soon," Mike instructed Goldie, trying to calm his excited dog.

Sassie gave Goldie a play bow and was also pulling her leash to greet Goldie.

Ruth and Mike moved to the Large Group Instruction Room, and when they got there, they released the dogs. As they ran free in this area, the dogs played Chase and lots of Play fighting.

Jane had spotted Mike and decided to invite him to join their meeting, "We usually have our meeting around this time. Mike, why don't you join us, and we can have our talk in the Large Group Instruction Room. I'll get the coffee made, and I believe we have a breakfast cake we can dig into."

Donald had begun working in the cat area, and Ruth found him washing their water bowls.

"Jane wants to call our meeting together in the Large Group Room in ten minutes. Will you be finished in time?"

Donald nodded yes. He quickly put away his things and made his way there.

There was a large table with several chairs in one corner of the room. The smell of coffee filled the air, and the breakfast cake had already been cut.

As they got their coffee and sat down, Jane began to speak, "First, let me thank Mike for joining us this morning. It is always good to have extra ideas whenever we meet. Donald, you brought up a concern that I believe we should address today. Would you tell us your thoughts?"

Donald began by saying, "I'm not comfortable with our method of animal adoption for the following reasons:

1) We do not have an official animal adoption form.

2) We have no way to contact those who have adopted our animals if for some reason we might need to.

Understanding Sassie II

3) There are no home visits or background questions that will reveal the home situation for our adopted animals."

Ruth jumped in to say, "I just got a call from Millie that I feel is connected to this concern. She said that today's newspaper had an article described a person who may have been stealing our local animals."

Jane felt that she needed to explain the reasoning behind the shelter adoption policy, "We've been able to have more animals adopted when we let them go home immediately with the people that selected them. Why should we make the adoption more difficult?"

Mike responded, "I've found a number of the animals that I knew had previously been brought to the shelter running free again. Sometimes they are in an unsuitable area, and sometimes they have been in situations that are dangerous. If we had a way of checking the names of those who adopted these animals, we might be able to penalize those owners. I like the idea of a home visit. I also believe that an application with some good questions will help us place our animals into a responsible forever home."

Ruth added, "If there is a person using animals for a bad reason, are we enabling that person freely to use the animal as they chose? We are supposed to be caretakers of these animals. I believe we are responsible for looking at the highest good for them."

Donald jumped in and added, "That's part of my

concern. What kind of caretakers would we be if we only want to unload our animals and not be sure they would go to caring and loving homes?"

Jane thought for a moment; she could see that the team had brought up some good points. "Okay, let's create an application form. If someone wishes to adopt one of our animals, they will be required to fill out this form. I think it is also a good idea to have a home visit. I'll put all adoptions on hold for at least 24 hours until we get this application ready for use. Donald, could you draft an application for us to approve by tomorrow morning?"

Donald gave a nod of assent, and Jane continued, "Are there any other topics we need to address at this time?" When no one brought forth a topic, Jane stood up and announced, "Let's get back to work."

Getting up from her seat, Ruth asked Mike, "Would you like to leave Goldie here for the afternoon? Sassie always seems to enjoy seeing Goldie again, and it will take Sassie's mind off Mom."

Mike smiled and said, "I know Goldie would enjoy more time with Sassie. Are you sure she would not be a problem?"

Ruth laughed and said, "No way. I enjoy having her here."

Mike then asked, "How is your mom?"

Ruth sighed and said, "She seems to be weak, but the doctor is unsure of what is causing this situation. I'm hoping the tests today will give us some answers. Thank you for asking."

As Mike was leaving, Ruth saw Donald approaching her. He was holding a clipboard; he looked like a man with a mission. "I've been working on the Shelter Adoption Form and I'm just not sure if I'm asking the right questions," he said as he approached Ruth. "I've made the home visit a mandatory item, but I'd like to get more information about a person's experience with animals and if they have a fenced-in back yard."

"That sounds good," Millie responded. She added, "How about questions like: 'Do you have children? What are their ages? Where will the animal sleep at night? Are there other animals in the home?'"

Donald liked Ruth's questions and added them to his notes. He said to Ruth, "Yes, that's exactly what I'm looking for. I'll type up a draft of the form and see what Jane thinks."

Donald stopped, looked at Ruth and saw the concern in her eyes. He knew that she was thinking about their mom, "Mom is in good hands at the hospital. Have you heard from the doctor yet?" He put his arm around Ruth.

Once again, Ruth was grateful for her big brother and his caring attitude. "No call yet, but it is still early in the day. Think I'll head for my office and get some paperwork done."

Unnoticed, Goldie and Sassie had been following Ruth. When she headed to her office, she had left the door open; the two dogs quietly climbed up onto the large and welcoming sofa.

The sofa and the large bookcase beside the sofa were Ruth's favorite parts of her office. The computer kept Ruth busy, but when she felt down or sad, the books and the sofa seemed to soothe and comfort her.

Ruth had been concentrating on the computer work. When the phone rang, she jumped. It also surprised the dogs, and they let out irritated barks. For the first time, Ruth noticed the dogs were in her office.

Their faces seemed to be saying, "We're most unhappy about that sound that woke us up!" Ruth began to laugh at them. They tucked their noses under their tails and decided to settle back to sleep.

Answering the phone with a "Hello," she recognized the doctor's voice.

"Good afternoon, Ruth. I was unable to determine the cause of your mom's fatigue. I would like to keep her in the hospital for at least another day and do some more testing. May I have your permission to keep her for at least another day?"

Ruth was shaking her head yes, then realized that the doctor could not see her.

Finding her voice, she replied, "Okay," then added, "please let me know if you discover anything." The doctor had already disconnected.

Ruth slowly hung up the phone. She became lost in thought, lost in worry.

She stared at the computer screen and saw her mother's face staring back at her. When she blinked, she realized what she was seeing was not her mom but her own face.

Still upset, she got up, went to the sofa, and took a comforting cuddle with the dogs. The dogs moved to accommodate Ruth, and love was given and received as they cuddled.

6

PUPPY PLAY DAY

The Riverview Animal Shelter was a very large building. The inside had recently been renovated but the outside still had the old-fashioned brickwork. Around the outside of the shelter there were several trees that provided not only color and delightful smells in the spring but fruit in the late summer and early fall. Millie had arrived early for the Puppy Play Day event. She wanted to have a moment to admire the fruit trees that were now in full bloom. Today she had stopped to watch the honey bees that nestled deep into each blossom.

When Millie entered the building, she was greeted by Jane, "Where's Goldie?" Jane asked.

"Mike will be bringing her," Millie answered, "that way he can work with Goldie, and it will leave me free to help the puppy owners with their questions as well as provide for me the freedom to give explanations as needed."

Jane announced, "I'm hoping for a good turn-out tonight. However, it might only be our regular group. I will have the basic hand-out rules available if we should get some 'newbies.'"

Millie smiled at Jane and remarked, "You always have this event under control. It's your planning and work that makes this time fun for puppies and humans alike. My sides seem to ache from laughing every time I leave this event."

Jane gave her a big grin and had to agree with Millie's hurting sides. "Yes, we laugh so much at the puppy antics that we all seem to go home with side cramps." Jane continued, "I found a new dog playtime game and made a copy for you to read. It's 'The Recall Game.' Could you read it over and see if it might be a good hand-out for tonight?"

Millie took the sheet from Jane and began to read.

Jane began to walk to the Large Group Instruction Room.

Millie had started to follow Jane, but because she had gone to this room many, many times, she thought, *no need to concentrate on directions. I'll just put my brain on human auto-pilot.*

Millie entered the large room and went to one of the many chairs that had already been set up for the puppy play time. Most were located by puppy Hide-a-ways.

Jane had walked over to talk to Donald, who had been setting up a few extra chairs. "It looks good to go. You've done an excellent job. I'm not surprised; you are a methodical person."

Jane heard Millie call her name; when she turned, Millie was motioning to Jane to come to her. With a wave to Donald, Jane moved to be by Millie.

"I like it," Millie said and then added, "the Recall Game is like teaching the Come with play. This is a great way to re-enforce the Come. I believe it will be a wonderful hand-out for tonight!"

Jane had taken the sheet from Millie and was on her way to the copier before Millie had a chance to finish her compliment.

Having finished the setup, Donald was now re-checking the "Hide-a-ways." He noticed Millie and commented, "Hi, Millie, I thought you were going to bring Goldie."

Millie explained that Mike would be bringing Goldie soon. Donald continued with some more questions. "Does the room look okay? Do you see anything I might have forgotten?"

"No," Millie responded, "I think you have got it all covered. I even see a few new dog toys."

She liked Donald. He was helpful, kind, and considerate to both humans and animals. Last year, Donald and Ruth had discovered that Valerie, Ruth's mom, was also Donald's birth mother. Ruth and Donald had become a happy and fun team at the shelter.

Millie had noticed a few changes in the Hide-a-ways. "Donald, I compliment you on your ideas for

Understanding Sassie II

these safe puppy Hide-a-ways. The improvements are very good. I am impressed."

Donald looked at his feet as he said, "Give the credit to Jane. She likes to tell me about her concerns. I only give her some ideas. Jane always encourages me to give my ideas a try. I must admit that some of the ideas have sent me to the library to do even more research."

Peg and Patrick usually were the first ones attending the Puppy Play Day. Tonight was no exception. They knew the routine. They walked their puppies to their usual chairs and quietly talked as they waited for the others to arrive.

Patrick looked at Peg and whispered, "Want to hear my newest dog joke?" Millie nodded and began to smile.

"Two neighbors, good hunting buddies, had been working in their garden when one said, 'Nice sunny day, neighbor.'

"The negative neighbor replied, 'If the sun keeps shining, it will begin to burn the crops.'

"The next day there was a soft rain, and once again both neighbors were out in the garden. The positive neighbor said, 'Isn't this gentle rain great for the plants?'

"The negative neighbor looked up at the sky and declared, 'If this continues, it will flood the garden and my crop will rot.'

"The positive neighbor decided to bring his well-trained dog with him to their upcoming hunting trip.

He'll have to say something nice about what my dog can do, he thought. They took the boat out, and it was not long before they saw ducks flying overhead. Shots were fired, and one duck fell to the water.

"Sending the dog to fetch the bird, they watched the dog step out of the boat and walk on the water. He went over to the bird and gently grabbed it. Then he walked on the water and stepped back into the boat. As the dog got back into the boat, the friendly neighbor asked his not-so-friendly friend, 'Well, what do you think of that?'

"His downbeat friend replied, 'Your dog can't swim, can he?'"

Peg started giggling. "Where do you find all these jokes?"

The excitement in the room began to build as the other puppies arrived with their people. Some of the puppies were staring at a specific toy that they would like to claim as their own.

The last team to arrive was Mike and Goldie. When Pal and Lady spotted Goldie, they each barked. Goldie began to pull her leash in their direction. This surprised Mike because she usually was not one to pull on the leash. "Goldie, relax!" he said and then added, "Sit. Stay."

Everyone turned to Millie as she began her talk.

She gave a quick review of the rules and an explanation of the presence of Goldie, the adult dog. "Usually, no older dogs have been allowed in the Puppy Play Day fun. I am making an exception for

Goldie," Millie explained, "who will be a positive example for the puppies. Goldie not only has good manners, she will also be patient with the puppies.

"Remember that the Hide-a-ways, that are near the chairs, are used to give your puppies a safe place to hide. There should only be one puppy per Hide-a-way. Let the puppy chose whatever he wants to do. He may hide, look out and watch, or he may choose to come out and play."

"At this time, release your dogs," Millie announced.

Pal and Lady ran towards Goldie and gave a quick Play Bow to her. Then they immediately began a game of Chase. As Goldie, Lady, and Pal frolicked with each other, some of other puppies were playing with the many toys that had been scattered about.

Mike turned to Millie and said, "Wow! Those Golden puppies are playing with Goldie like they know her."

"Yes," Millie agreed. "They are acting like best friends!"

Goldie had begun to help some of the shy puppies gain confidence. She would grab a toy and shake it near the Hide-a-ways where one of the puppies was hiding. She'd then do a Play Bow and run away. This was to encourage the puppy to chase her. Sometimes she'd do a sniff and pretend to be interested in something. Usually this would encourage the puppy to see what it was that she was interested in.

Goldie never rushed a shy puppy. It was as though she knew they wanted to play but were also a little scared of the new circumstance. She continued to do a good job of teaching the shy puppies that they were safe and could have fun playing with the other puppies.

As the hour-long play was coming to an end, many of the puppies began to tire.

Millie started her departure instructions with an important announcement. "Could I have your attention please? I'd like to give a warning before you leave tonight. Please always keep a close eye on your dogs. In today's newspaper there was an article that said that there may be a dog thief in the area. Please leash your dogs at this time and remember to respect each other's space as you leave."

When Millie mentioned the words, "dog thief," Pat and Peg looked at each other and agreed that they needed to talk to Millie. "Miss Millie," they began, "earlier this spring we had Pal and Lady play with a group of dogs in the Riverview Park tennis area.

"We noticed a man staring at the dogs. There was something disturbing about how he was acting. I told Patrick I was glad we stayed with the dogs!"

Peg paused and then took a better look at Millie. "Wait a minute," Peg said, "I saw you there! Was that your wedding celebration?"

Millie smiled at the teenagers, "Yes, we did have a dog play area in the tennis court at our wedding.

Understanding Sassie II

I'm now realizing that Goldie met Lady and Pal at that time."

Millie continued, "Thank you for sharing your observation with me. Let's keep our eyes open, and if we see anything unusual, we'll be sure to tell the police."

7

PSYCH

It was Monday, and Psych decided that today might be a good day to check out the animals at the Riverview Animal Shelter.

Let's see, the flyer said the hours were 10 a.m. to 4 p.m. My work here is done, and I'm free to do as I wish until late this afternoon. It's 10 a.m. now, he thought as he looked at his watch. *It would be a good time to visit the Riverview Animal Shelter and get me a bait dog or two for my young dogs' fight training.*

He jumped into his ten-year-old Ford pickup and began his trip to the shelter.

As he took his time looking over the dogs at the Riverview shelter, he found a few dogs that looked interesting. One small mixed-breed was growling and full of energy. *Yep*, Psych thought, *that one might be perfect.*

When he approached the area for finalizing

a dog adoption, he was surprised to see the clerk hand him an application form.

"What's this?" Psych asked.

"It's the application form for adoption," the clerk replied.

"I just want a dog!" Psych yelled, "I'm not doing no paperwork!" Then he demanded, "I want to see your supervisor!"

Jane was called. When she came to the dog adoption desk, she asked, "Is there a problem here?"

Angry, Psych answered, "I'm being told that I need to fill out an application form and have a home visit before I take a dog to my home!"

"I'm sorry, sir," Jane explained, "we have instituted a new adoption policy, and we now require a completed adoption application form and a home visit."

"Are you saying that I can't take a dog home today?" Psych waved a pamphlet in Jane's face and continued, "That is not what your pamphlet says!"

Jane apologized and repeated, "We've instituted some new adoption procedures and are in the process of updating our pamphlets. You are free to choose an animal, but you will still need to fill out this application. I'm sure we could expedite the home visit and possibly have you pick up tomorrow the dog you have chosen."

Grumbling, Psych grabbed the application and walked toward the exit.

"Sir," Jane called to Psych's back, "we will need a completed application before we can process your request for a dog."

Her words were ignored as Psych headed for the parking lot. "Damn new rules!" Psych said under his breath. "It was a bad idea to attempt to get a dog from here!"

Gunning the truck's engine, he thought about the dogs that he had already stolen. They had been in areas where dogs were unsupervised and often neglected. Upset and still angry, he decided that he needed a drink! *Anyways, I think this hot and sticky day is a good day for a beer.*

He took the turn into town and headed for the Riverview Village Bar.

Mike seldom went to the Riverview Village Bar, but when his friends asked him to join them, he decided to go. He did like the idea of having a cold beer on such a hot day.

Mike and his pals entered the bar; several of the locals were playing poker. By the looks of the amount of cash on the table, it was a high-stakes game.

There was music playing, but Mike did not recognize any of the songs. He did notice that the music was loud.

Speaking over the music, Mike told the bartender, "Give me and each of my buddies a beer."

Mike paid the bartender. One of the locals yelled, "Hi, Mike! How's the wife?"

Others were more interested in the disappearance

Understanding Sassie II

of some local dogs. One asked, "Have you found any of the missing dogs?"

Mike was not sure he wanted to talk about his gruesome discovery concerning one of the missing dogs.

He tried to change the subject, "Man! Today is one very hot day!"

He moved to a window table and sat down. He just wanted to take a long drink of his cold beer and relax.

His hope of not answering the missing-dogs question was not to be fulfilled. Another patron asked, "Hey, Mike, what do you know about the missing dogs?"

Mike wanted to be honest, but he also did not want to describe what he had found concerning the missing dogs. He decided to say that he had found one of the missing dogs, dead, but would not explain nor describe the dog's condition.

He reported, "You know how it is. A dog chases an animal across a road, and a car hits the dog. Sometimes dogs are not familiar with fast-moving road traffic and are accidentally killed."

"Okay, Mike, thanks for the information," came the reply.

Mike let out a quiet sigh of relief, thankful that this answer satisfied the missing-dog question.

Suddenly, there was an explosive crash.

At the sound, Mike threw his table onto its side; he and his buddies took cover behind it.

Mike drew his Animal Control Officer pistol but then realized that it was only a fist-fight, with no need for gunfire.

A man ran out of the bathroom to see what had created all the noise. His timing resulted in his head becoming connected with a flying chair.

The poker table had been flipped onto the floor; chairs had been used as battering rams, causing destruction throughout much of the area.

There resounded shouts of "cheater," "crook," and "you're stacking the deck!" as well as the sound of fist-fighting. The noise drew everyone's attention to the origin of the ruckus, the battling poker players.

Psych had entered the Village Bar just as the noise began. Somehow, he was able to side-step the disaster and order a beer from the bartender. When the beer came, Psych asked, "Is fighting a regular occurrence here?"

"Sometimes" was the bartender's vague reply.

Psych took a large swallow of beer and thought to himself, *Interesting. Everyone here seems to enjoy watching a fight. I wonder if they would be as interested in watching a good dog-fight?*

8

DONALD, RUTH, AND THE FARM

Donald had been living in a section of the farmhouse that belonged to his birth mother, Valerie. He ate his meals with Ruth and Valerie. Now that Valerie had been in the hospital for over a week, Ruth and Donald were becoming more and more concerned about their mother.

They requested that the doctor meet them that afternoon at their mother's bedside.

Ruth had brought Sassie, Valerie's Diabetic Service Dog, with her. Sassie kissed Valerie's hand and nudged her elbow, but Valerie had paid no attention to her dog.

When Donald entered wearing a red nose and a purple wig, he was hoping to get Valerie to smile. He even told her a silly joke. It was one that always made Valerie laugh, but this time she only gave a blank stare at Donald.

The doctor had seen Sassie's and Donald's

attempts to engage Valerie and Valerie's failure to respond. He decided to order a few neurological tests. He also concluded he should do an MRI of Valerie's brain. Asking Ruth and Donald for permission to do another workup on Valerie, he received their permission for the additional testing.

"I'll schedule the tests and an MRI for tomorrow, and I will call you as soon as I get the results," the doctor said as he left Valerie's room.

Ruth put Sassie into her car and asked Donald to follow her home. When they arrived, they quietly walked into the house. "Donald," Ruth began, "it's going to be difficult to wait until the doctor calls tomorrow!"

"I agree," Donald responded, "but maybe there is something we can do to distract us and keep us busy."

"That seems impossible,' Ruth claimed, and then asked, "what are you suggesting?"

"Our mom told me that you are a champion Scrabble player. Is that true?"

"Yes," Ruth said with a big smile, "I've entered a number of prize tournaments and won every one!" Then she added proudly, "No one has ever bested me in a game of Scrabble!"

Donald replied, "Well, you never have played Scrabble against me!"

Ruth looked at Donald. She asked, in disbelief, "Are you really telling me that you believe you can win against me at Scrabble?"

"Maybe," Donald replied, "but can you think of a better way to forget our worries?" The game began, and Ruth soon discovered that Donald was an excellent Scrabble player.

When the morning sun peaked into their living-room window, it revealed two sleepy people tied in Scrabble points.

"I need a break. Let's get something to eat," Ruth said as she stood up to stretch her legs.

"That's a good idea," Donald replied. "I'll make the coffee."

As Donald was making the coffee, Ruth heated some blueberry muffins. Ruth looked at Donald with a new respect and said, "I've never competed with a challenger as good as you! Where did you learn to be such a good Scrabble player?"

Donald started to explain but was interrupted by the ringing telephone.

Ruth ran to the phone. "I hope it's a call from the hospital." She picked up the telephone. "Hello."

Ruth recognized the doctor's voice when he replied, "The MRI scan has shown a tumor in a sensitive part of Valerie's brain. This tumor is causing her weakness and loss of memory. It would be too dangerous to try to get a biopsy of this growth. Surgery to remove this large tumor would also be out of the question. The shape of the growth looks to be cancer. I'm sorry to report that I believe she will soon need round-the-clock care and supervision. She may even slip into a coma."

Not willing to listen any more to the devastating news, Ruth handed the phone to Donald and collapsed in a nearby chair.

The doctor repeated the information to Donald and added, "I can make arrangements to move her to a facility that specializes in the care of patients like your mom. Would you like me to look into this for you?"

Donald said, "Yes, but Ruth and I will make the final decision on Valerie's future."

The next day Valerie did slip into a coma. She died two days later. Ruth asked the doctor for permission to bring Sassie to the hospital and let her say good-bye. Permission was granted. Sassie approached the bed, and with a sniff, the dog seemed to understand that Valerie was no longer alive.

It was a sad time for Donald and Ruth. Ruth took comfort in saying, "Valerie had lived 90 good years."

Donald was grateful for the fact that he had finally found Valerie, his birth mother, and that he was able to get to know her as a wonderful person.

It was about a month after the funeral that the family lawyer called Donald and Ruth to a meeting in his office. He was going to read the will.

Ruth and Donald were surprised to hear that the farm had been left equally to each of them. *Mom must have created this will recently, right after Mary died in that auto crash*, Ruth thought. Mary had been her much older sister. Mary lived out of state and had come to visit them about six months ago.

The auto crash occurred when she was traveling home.

Ruth and Donald just looked at each other. *Can we handle the work of a large farm?* seemed to be the unspoken question in their eyes.

There were no longer any animals on the farm; half of the original 200 acres had been sold. Repairs and the upkeep would still be big responsibilities. They had been doing some of the farm work, but that was after asking Valerie for advice and directions.

"Maybe it would be wise to keep a normal routine on the farm until we understand the best future for all this," Donald suggested. Ruth agreed; Donald added, "I already have been mending the breaks in the fences and have repaired some of the equipment."

"Yes," Ruth decided, "that sounds like the best solution for us, for now." Thus, the routine began... with Ruth in charge of "inside" chores and Donald in charge of "outside" chores.

9

DONALD, RUTH, AND THE CAT

Donald and Ruth continued to work at the shelter. He loved working with all the animals, and he especially liked the independent attitude of the cats. The sound of their purring when they were happy always brought a smile to his face.

When a young cat, a stray, had been brought to the shelter, she was found to be hungry for attention. She decided to adopt Donald. Donald enjoyed this pretty cat; he started calling her, "Pretty Girl."

Whenever Donald entered the cat area, Pretty Girl would begin crying until Donald visited her. If he left to work in another area, she would again begin crying until he returned to her area. Deciding that it would be okay for her to be free in the cat's area, as he worked, he let her roam freely there.

Pretty Girl followed Donald everywhere. She hopped up onto the sink and watched him wash the cat bowls. She rubbed against his legs as he replaced the litter boxes with fresh, clean-smelling litter. Donald talked to her constantly as he was working. She would sing her purr-like song in reply.

With Ruth's blessing, he filed the paperwork to adopt Pretty Girl. She became part of the farm family. She still followed him everywhere, but her domain was restricted to inside the house.

"You are going to be a house cat," Donald explained to her, "but you'll be safer that way."

Pretty Girl decided that her job at night was to hop up onto Donald's bed and purr her special song for him until he fell asleep.

Being on the farm was wholly unlike life in New York City. Donald seemed to find peace and relaxation whenever he wandered around the farm. As he explored Mother Nature, he discovered beauty...and some unknown living things. The unknowns sent him to the Riverview library to obtain information.

There was a large forest in one area of the farm. Here Donald discovered a flower that was named a "lady slipper." When he went to the library to research wild flowers, he was surprised to know that the lady slipper was so rare it had laws protecting it.

The forest often held special surprises for Donald. He saw animals that he had never seen in New York City, where he had lived for over twenty years before moving to Upper New York State. The Riverview library became his "answers, please" place to go. Each new farm experience became an exciting library treasure hunt.

Donald shared a very special forest surprise with Jane. He began, "One beautiful day, I had been daydreaming as I was sitting on a large fallen tree. I heard a soft noise. In front of me a young deer appeared. I didn't dare move. As I watched the deer, I realized that the animal was a youngster. She was moving forward at a cautious speed. It was then that I heard a squirrel, high in a pine tree, dislodge a twig. The noise was enough to spook the deer. As I looked back to the spot where the young deer had stood, I started to shake my head in wonder as I asked myself, had I really seen that beautiful animal?"

Donald also enjoyed listening to the large variety of bird calls. Some birds sang a melody that would sound much like its name. Chick-a-dee-dee-dee was one of these birds.

It always seemed to be so peaceful being with Mother Nature. He did realize that it was never absolutely quiet, but because it was so unlike the sounds of the big city, the forest sounds always managed to soothe his anxiety and put his troubling thoughts into perspective.

The wind in this farm's river valley always seemed to be gentle, almost the light tickle of a soft feather. The smells carried by the wind could bring the hint of cut grass or even the scent of wild flowers. The river would sing a melody of song as it struggled over the rocks and the many tree branches that disturbed its path. Each day with Mother Nature was not only an adventure but a special memory.

On a day Donald was driving to the farm from Riverview Animal Shelter, he began to daydream about his life and how different it was from his life in New York City. He turned right instead of left and began traveling in the wrong direction. He did not discover his mistake until he had gone over a mile down this road.

What is that? He said to himself. He suddenly realized that the scenery was unfamiliar. At the same time, he realized he was lost.

The mysterious scenery encouraged him to go farther and investigate the field ahead. He kept looking at strange white lumps that looked like moving piles of snow. "I've never seen anything like this!" he said.

Drawing closer to the area, he realized the white things were animals grazing. He pulled his vehicle to the side of the road to investigate these four-legged fluffs of cotton.

I think these are sheep. He spotted a dog lying quietly in the grass near them. The Border Collie had been studying Donald.

When a dog lies down near the herd, it calms the sheep; this Donald discovered when he began to research sheep at the library.

Because the dog decided that Donald was not a threat to the sheep, the dog made no attempt to get up and move the flock.

Donald watched the sheep for a long time. He was fascinated with these gentle animals and was in no hurry to move from this peaceful scene.

When he finally looked at his watch, he was surprised at the time. *I'd better get to the farm or I'll be late for supper. Ruth wants to have supper promptly at 5:00 p.m. and it is 4:40 now!*

The car's tires created a pair of deep tracks as he gunned the motor and drove away. He did manage to get to the farm by 4:59 p.m. Racing into the kitchen, he saw that Ruth had already set the table.

When she saw Donald, she pointed at the old-fashioned wall clock. "You're late!" Ruth announced, sounding annoyed.

"I'm sorry," Donald replied and added, "I'll be there as soon as I wash my hands."

Ruth began to dish food onto their plates as soon as Donald sat down.

"As you know, Sassie had her annual check-up with the veterinarian today. He said that she is healthy." Ruth continued to talk about Sassie's check-up, adding, "However, he did say that it might be wise for her to lose a few pounds."

Donald replied with his mouth half-full, "I don't think she's too heavy!"

Ruth was going to say, "Donald, don't talk with your mouth full," but then remembered how much she hated her mom's saying that. Instead, Ruth replied, "I agree, but it might be wise to heed the vet and to plan more exercise for her."

Understanding Sassie II

Donald thought for a minute. "I think she needs a new job. The library is looking for dogs that children can read to. I'm sure that Sassie could easily get her Therapy Dog certification. She loves children, and she'd be wonderful for that job!"

Ruth nodded yes. "That's a great idea. I'll look into it."

10

JANE, MILLIE, AND RUTH

Millie had been spending more time at the shelter. She believed that working with some of the shelter dogs could help them become more adoptable.

She enjoyed walking the shelter's dogs and found that her walking techniques were being very successful. She would encourage them to walk close to her by randomly giving super-good treats. She was also testing some of the behavior modifications she had had learned in college. Between Millie's training and the new adoption rules, the number of repeat captives had been reduced to almost zero.

Mike was very happy to see that more of the animals had found their forever homes.

Millie and Mike spent many evenings sharing stories about their daily experiences. "That Pit Bull that you brought in today," Millie shared, "was so jumpy and terrified of women."

Mike acknowledged her observations and added, "I'm glad I was able to capture her and bring her to the shelter. I knew you would be the one who could help her, if there was any hope for a normal life for her."

"She is definitely a challenge," Millie said, "and, I do love challenges. I finally got her to relax by ignoring her and accidently dropping tasty treats into her area. She thought I was clumsy, but she could cope with a clumsy woman. The Pit Bull finally relaxed whenever I walked by and seemed to be looking for those accidental and delicious treats."

"Keep it up, Honey!" Mike encouraged her. "She did seem to look for my gentle touch, and I felt so sad for her. That's when I realized that she did not seem to fear men."

Millie and Ruth had been planning to start some dog training classes and decided to begin with the Puppy Socialization class. The owner of any puppy adopted from the Riverview Animal Shelter or any puppy that attends Puppy Play dates on a regular basis would only be charged 50% of the full five-week fee. It was scheduled to begin on a Wednesday evening in twelve days.

Jane, the shelter supervisor, had spent all morning working on the shelter's budget. *We're in the black!* Jane thought. She had checked her figures several times and was happy with the totals. *Adoptions have increased, and with Millie's and Ruth's ideas about dog training, I believe I can afford to give some extra benefits to the volunteers. I will also be able to offer Millie a part-time salary.*

Jane also remembered that Ruth had been talking about her dream of becoming a Certified Professional Dog Trainer. It was an expensive dream, and Ruth had felt she could not afford to pursue her dream at that time. Jane thought, *I can give Ruth a scholarship for her educational expenses.*

Jane believed that Millie's knowledge was too valuable to have someone take her away from her work at the shelter and a CPDT-educated dog trainer would be invaluable at the shelter.

I believe a scholarship will be well worth the expenditure, and the salary for Millie may keep her working at the shelter, she decided.

Voicing her decision, she announced to herself, "I'll talk to them today."

Jane decided that now would be a good time to get a cup of coffee. Unknown to Jane, Millie and Ruth had been talking in the break room. When Jane saw them, she poured herself a cup of coffee and joined them at their table.

They welcomed Jane to their table; they could tell that she wanted to say something to them.

"I've got some good news for both of you," Jane began. "Millie, how would you like a part-time job at the shelter?"

Millie looked puzzled and said, "But I already am working a part-time job here."

Smiling, Jane responded, "No, I mean a paid part-time job."

Millie's mouth dropped open, "You want to pay me for something I enjoy doing voluntarily?"

Jane explained, "I just don't want you to work for someone else. You are way too valuable to me."

"Wow!" was all Millie could say.

Jane then turned to Ruth, "Ruth, I know you want to become a CPDT, a Certified Professional Dog Trainer. I would like to give you a scholarship to help with the expenses as you earn this title."

Stunned, Ruth also said, "Wow!"

Jane got up from her seat, mission accomplished, and started to leave with her coffee; she added, "I'll draw up the paperwork, and we'll talk again later."

Millie and Ruth looked at each other and realized the wonderful gifts Jane had just given to them. Millie thought, *this will help to pay off my student loans. I can't wait to tell Mike!*

Ruth almost danced in her seat when she realized her dream of becoming a Certified Professional Dog Trainer was doable. She thought, I *can't wait to tell Donald!*

As they congratulated each other, they realized that they still needed to continue planning the curriculum for the upcoming Puppy Socialization class.

Ruth asked, "Did we decide to give the puppies any free play time?"

Millie looked down at her notes and replied, "Maybe we might do that near the end. I'm not sure about this. It might be a good reward, but I also know they will be tired."

Ruth then asked, "Should we demonstrate some of the basic safety tips?" She added, "I'd like to talk about my positive-hand-near-the-bowl method."

Millie agreed and said, "I know you trained Sassie with that method, and I believe it will help to prevent accidental biting when a dog is eating food."

When Ruth looked at her watch, she realized that their break time was over. She said, "I believe we both have some good ideas. Let's write down whatever we might want to add to the training sessions and then compare notes on Monday."

Millie got up, replying, "Sounds like a good plan. That will give us the weekend to create our lists of thoughts. On Monday we'll plan to compare notes."

11

THE LIBRARY

On Saturday afternoon Ruth had taken Sassie to a Therapy Dog group testing. Ruth believed that Sassie could easily pass the testing challenges, and she did. After sending the paperwork to register Sassie for her Therapy Dog identification tag, Ruth decided that she would like to visit the Riverview Library and talk to the librarian about the Reading to a Dog Program.

"Donald, were you going to the library today?" Ruth asked. When Donald nodded his head yes, Ruth continued, "Can I ride along with you when you go?"

Donald replied, "Sure." Then he told Ruth, "I plan on spending about an hour to do research. Will that be enough time for whatever you plan to do?"

"Yes," Ruth responded, "I think that will be more than enough time, but I can keep busy until you're ready to leave."

An hour later they were traveling to the library.

Donald introduced Ruth to the librarian and then left to do his research. "What can I do for you?" the librarian asked.

"Donald mentioned that there was a Read to Your Dog Program, and that you were looking for more dogs that youngsters could read to," Ruth said and then continued, "my dog, Sassie, has passed the Therapy Dog test, and I'd like to have her participate in this program."

The librarian smiled and reached for a prepared packet. "Here is some information on the reading program; it also contains a form which you will need to complete before your dog can participate in this program. Please look over the information, and if you have any questions, I would be happy to answer them for you." The librarian then handed the packet to Ruth.

Taking the packet, Ruth began to look for a place to relax and read. She noticed that this library was bigger than most village libraries. It had been built with money from, and at the direction of, a well-known historian, one who knew the value of a good library. He insisted on a large research section with up-to-date computers and up-to-date books. He was also thinking of his grandchildren when he donated additional funds for a good children's section in this library. When the historian died, he donated his entire personal book collection to the Riverview Library. This created a library that was superior to libraries found in many of the bigger cities.

Ruth had found an area perfect for both relaxing

Understanding Sassie II

and reading. She quickly became absorbed in reading this well-prepared packet.

Meanwhile Donald had found several books that he wanted to bring home for additional reading and further research. He was now at the book check-out desk with a stack of books in his rolling cart. Donald frequently used his collapsible rolling cart whenever he visited the library. As each book was checked out, he carefully placed it into his sturdy cart.

Donald noticed a schedule had been posted near-by with the times and dates for the Read to Your Dog Program. Then he realized Ruth was studying this schedule. Ruth had already filled out an application for Sassie and had given it to the librarian. When Ruth asked her about a suggestion for Sassie's possible reading assignment, the librarian suggested that Sassie could come tomorrow and meet some of the young readers. Ruth liked the suggestion and agreed to come.

When Ruth looked up from the dog's reading schedule, she realized that Donald was heading toward the library door exit. With a loud whisper she said, "Donald, wait for me!"

Donald did not hear her. His thoughts were only about his library books. *I can't wait to get home and spread out my library books.*

Ruth recognized Donald was excited. She knew he just wanted to go home and begin digging for the treasure that he knew would be buried within the books' covers.

12

A BATH AND A HURRICANE

When Donald and Ruth got home from the library, Ruth knew that Donald would go directly to his room and work with the books he had just gotten.

Sassie had been teasing Ruth to play catch with one of her toys. Ruth gave in and played for a little while but then realized that if Sassie was going to the library tomorrow, she would need a bath today.

Sassie liked bath-time because of the special treats she got during it. She also had a few special bath toys that she would only be able to play with during bath-time. Ruth set out the bath things and began playing with her and rewarding her as she carefully soaped Sassie's long hair.

Ruth was getting wet, too; she laughed and said to Sassie, "You are having fun not only because you have your special toys, but I let you jump in and out of the tub. I guess I'm having a bath right along with you!"

Ruth also recognized that after Sassie's bath she would need to do a major bathroom clean-up. When the bath was done, Ruth gave Sassie a good rub-down and massage. This also gave Ruth a good chance to check Sassie's skin and hair.

"I'll leave most of the brushing for tomorrow, but I do want to eliminate the snarls and matted hair areas," she told Sassie while she brushed.

After the major bathroom clean-up, Ruth made a quick-and-easy supper of soup and sandwiches. Donald stayed at the table to eat the soup but then retreated to his room with his sandwich.

"Well, Sassie, I guess it's just you and me this evening. Come join me on the sofa and let's see what's on the news."

"We come on the air with Breaking News this evening!" Ruth turned up the television's volume, "There is a report of a Category Four hurricane just off the Gulf Coast. Many residents along the shore are being asked to evacuate."

Ruth thought, *I wonder if Jane has heard the news?* Reaching for the phone, she dialed Jane's number. *A hurricane could mean that we will be receiving many dogs and cats from the shelters in the hurricane evacuation area; we'd better prepare.*

Jane answered the call on the first ring.

"Have you heard the news about the Gulf Coast hurricane?" Ruth asked.

"Yes, I have," Jane replied. "They are waiting on the animal evacuation until they know exactly where the hurricane will make landfall. It's a good thing that our shelter is one of the ones that now have a low number of animals. We should be able to help if we are needed."

"That is good to know," Ruth replied and then proudly added, "speaking about something good, I want to share some good news with you! Sassie has been accepted to work in the Read to Dogs Program at the library. We're going tomorrow to meet some of the young readers."

Donald had just come out of his room to get a glass of milk from the kitchen when he heard Ruth talking to Jane.

"Hi, Jane," he yelled in Ruth's direction.

Ruth turned and said, "Why don't you tell her that yourself? You can also tell her about your research."

As Donald took the phone, he made an annoying face at Ruth. He wanted her to think he was upset for being pulled away from his research. He was glad for an opportunity to talk to Jane. "Hi, Jane," Donald said with a smile in his voice. "I'm really starting to understand a lot about Mother Nature and farm life."

Jane laughed at Donald's words and said, "What have you discovered?"

As soon as Donald had taken the phone and started to speak to Jane, Ruth turned to Sassie and said, "We might as well let them talk. They will be on the phone for hours."

On a distant abandoned farm, Psych was excited at the prospect of getting some bait dogs from the hurricane dog rescues. He had given his name to the rescue groups and said that he had room to shelter several dogs. *They'll be too busy to check on me and my location,* he thought. *I'd brought doctored photos that make my area look like the perfect foster home for any dog.*

Little did he realize that the Riverview Animal Shelter would have plans that would prove to be Psych's windfall's downfall.

13

READING TO SASSIE

The next morning, Ruth brushed Sassie's hair until it was shiny and silky soft. Sassie knew something special was going to happen, and she began to wiggle all over with excitement.

"You need to use your best manners today," Ruth told Sassie.

Sassie knew the word "manners" meant that she had to be extra good. She wagged her tail to let Ruth know that she understood and was promising to "be a good girl."

When Ruth parked in the library parking lot, Sassie waited for Ruth to attach a leash to her collar and then she walked politely up the library steps and into the building. Sassie heard children's voices and started to wiggle with excitement but when Ruth said "Relax," she lay down and watched quietly.

A little girl came over to Ruth and asked, "May I pet your dog?'

Understanding Sassie II

Ruth complimented her on her good manners and said, "Yes, you may pet my dog. Her name is Sassie."

The girl started to giggle and said, "That's what my dad says about me. He says I'm too sassy! My name is Sharon."

Ruth asked, "Are you here to read to a dog?"

"No", Sharon replied sadly, "my Dad said I should give others a chance to read. I'm a good reader but I would love to have a chance to read to one of the dogs. Daddy says that I should be polite and let others read to the dogs."

Ruth could see that Sharon really liked dogs; she wanted her to have a chance to spend some time with Sassie. "I tell you what," Ruth suggested, "Sassie will be spending a lot of time today listening to people read to her. She probably will need some exercise after being quiet for such a long time. There is a large lawn behind the library. It would be a good area for someone to play with Sassie. Why not have your Dad and you meet us there, and you can help Sassie get some exercise?"

Sharon replied, "Really? I'll ask my Dad to come to that lawn so that he can meet Sassie. If he gives me permission, I'd love to play with her."

Sharon seemed to dance a happy dance as she disappeared into the rows and rows of library books.

The librarian noticed Ruth and Sassie and came over to direct them to the "Read to the Dog" area. There were several students that had signed up to read who were already in the area. When they saw Sassie, they all wanted to pet her. Ruth gave each student permission to greet Sassie. As other students waited their turn, the librarian directed them to get a book for reading.

The dogs and students were then assigned their reading area. Sassie had managed to give every student at least one kiss and never stopped wagging her tail.

Ruth heard the librarian call each student by name and wondered, *how does she remember everyone's name?*

A few of the parents had lingered near the reading area and were quietly talking amongst themselves.

"I'm so grateful for this program!" a young mother was quietly telling the person sitting next to her. "My son has started to enjoy reading. His teacher said that she saw a big improvement in his reading skills."

It was fun to listen to their conversations, and Ruth liked the stories they told.

A friend of one of the Moms began to tell about her nature-loving dog. "The dog that your child is reading her story to looks a lot like my Sugar. I miss her every day. She was a small dog that loved to chase leaves and visit with the various animals that came to our yard. She seemed to be able to convince them that she would never harm them. I loved to watch her slowly approach a rabbit and see them

Understanding Sassie II

sniff noses. I even saw a baby deer come up to her. The fawn got a kiss from Sugar.

"It was a sad day when the Vet said that Sugar had cancer. I was heart-broken but I felt that I wanted her to continue to enjoy the outdoors. I made sure that she could continue to go outside. When she got too weak to walk around the yard, I would bring her to the porch and place her on a blanket as I sat near-by.

"Sugar loved to sniff the air. On this one day as she lay quietly, I wondered if she may have been saying good-bye to Mother Nature. My thoughts were confirmed when a rabbit came across the lawn and up to the porch steps. He let out a soft sound and then hopped up the steps to Sugar. They touched noses, and it was like the rabbit needed to say good-bye to his friend.

"What happened next was even more surprising. A deer came out of the bushes and right up to the porch. She then came onto the porch and touched noses with Sugar. Then both animals left. That night, Sugar died."

Ruth thought, *why is it so surprising to us when we realize just how much our animals understand someone's feelings?*

The story of Sugar inspired another mom to share her story about her dog, Sammy.

"Sammy is a good-sized dog. I'd been able to teach him that he was to always remain in the area near our home. There was a nearby grocery store that held many dog-tempting smells, but Sammy had been trained to ignore this temptation.

"On a day when I was looking out of the upstairs bedroom window, I saw Sammy sitting in front of the grocery store. The window was open. I yelled, 'Sammy, what are you doing? Come home this minute!'

"Sammy raced toward home. The garage door was open, and he thought that I had been inside that area. He stopped just before the open garage door. As he slowly peeked around the corner of the open door, he was acting as if he was saying, 'Here I am! I've been here the whole time.'

"Sammy did not realize that I had been watching all his actions from the upstairs window."

The reading time had concluded, and the librarian began to collect the books. As she called each student by name, she said, "See you next week." Ruth began to clip her leash to Sassie's collar when the librarian said, "I'd like to put Sassie on the schedule for Saturdays. That is the day when we usually need a larger number of dogs." Ruth nodded in agreement and then traveled to the library exit.

Once outside, Ruth headed toward the lawn behind the library.

14

SHARON AND SASSIE

As soon as Sharon saw Sassie, she began to run across the lawn, yelling, "Hi, Sassie!" Ruth smiled at the young girl's excitement. Ruth could feel Sassie tugging on her leash. Sassie was wagging her tail; she had recognized Sharon's voice. From her pocket, Ruth pulled Sassie's favorite play toy, the ball, and as soon as Sharon started to pet Sassie, Ruth passed the ball to her. Ruth unclipped Sassie's collar, and Sharon and Sassie ran off to play.

"I didn't know you owned a dog," Jim said. Ruth turned and recognized the boss from her old job at the Corporation.

"Jim, what are you doing here?" Ruth asked, surprised. They both started to talk at the same time and then stopped and began to laugh.

"Sharon is my daughter," Jim answered. "We often visit the library on the weekend. Is that your dog? Sharon has been talking about her for the last hour."

Ruth replied, "Yes, she's my Therapy Dog and I am bringing her here for the Read to Your Dog program. I adopted her when I was volunteering at the Riverview Animal Shelter." Ruth continued, "I didn't realize that you are married. Is your wife with you? Do you have any more children?"

Jim looked sad as he replied, "My wife died a month before I got promoted to the supervisory position at the Corporation. I believe that was the reason they gave me the promotion. The extra work kept me busy, and I could really use the extra income during that time. Sharon is my only child. That new position helped me to get through a rough time. Sharon has been able to bury herself in the library books. I believe that helped her to deal with her feelings, too."

Laughter came from Sharon as she danced around with Sassie. "I haven't heard Sharon laugh like that in a long, long time," Jim announced.

Ruth looked at Jim and for the first time began to realize why he had been so well liked at the Corporation.

"I'm sorry...." Ruth said in compassion to Jim. She felt shame as well and had a new understanding of how foolish she had been at the Corporation. "...I hope you'll forgive me for who I was back then."

Jim shook his head and said, "We learn from our

mistakes. That's how we grow. My motto has been that it is not a mistake if we learn from it!"

They gave each other a hug and called Sassie and Sharon to join them.

"I'm scheduled to bring Sassie to the Read to Your Dog program next Saturday. Sharon, would you like to make another date for playing with Sassie on Saturday?" Ruth asked this of Sharon but looked at Jim for the permission.

"Yes," Sharon answered quickly, while looking at her father for confirmation. Jim nodded his head, and as they started for the parking lot, Ruth began to tell Jim about the Riverview Animal Shelter and the impending Gulf Coast hurricane.

"There are at least two shelters in the evacuation area," Ruth explained. "Riverview Animal Shelter would need to bring a number of these animals up to our shelter. The biggest challenge for us will be the transportation of these animals from the Gulf Area to Upper New York State."

Jim smiled and said, "I can help you solve that problem."

Ruth continued to talk. She was so concerned about Riverview Animal Shelter's problems, she was only talking but not listening.

"My stepbrother, Donald, is preparing a computer program for the recording of all the information on each animal. Into each animal, we will be placing an identification chip that will also have a GPS-tracker component. We have been placing this chip into all our shelter animals and are now offering this service to the community. We felt that this would help with locating any lost dogs"

Jim realized that Ruth had not heard his offer of transportation help; he decided to repeat his offer, "Ruth, I can help you with your transportation problem."

Ruth heard what he said, but she couldn't believe what she had heard. "What did you say?" She stopped and turned to Jim.

"I said that I have a large private jet and can help you with the transporting of the Gulf Coast animals."

Ruth jumped up and gave Jim a big kiss. This surprised Jim, but he just smiled when Ruth began to apologize for her actions.

He was pleased to see Ruth so happy and excited and replied to her apologies by saying, "Give me the Riverview Animal Shelter Supervisor's phone number, and I'll take care of all the animal transportation concerns. Rest assured that the Gulf Coast animal evacuation will be successful."

15

GULF COAST EVACUATION

The evacuation of the Gulf Coast had begun. The Category Four hurricane was scheduled to make landfall within the hour. The Riverview Animal Shelter had already begun receiving some of the animals evacuated from the Gulf Coast.

The Gulf Coast shelters were well organized and had attached each animal's medical records to their transportation carriers. This enabled the team of veterinarians at Riverview Animal Shelter to evaluate each animal easily and provide any care needed. They were then microchipped with some information and a GPS tracker.

Donald was responsible for entering all the evacuation information into the Riverview Animal Shelter computer.

The Shelter had several foster families that had volunteered to take in some of the evacuated animals, helping to avoid overcrowding the shelter.

Psych realized that the Shelter had now been receiving many animals from the Gulf Coast. *I wonder how I can become a foster family for some of these animals,* he thought. *I wonder if I would be able to use a fake location and fake name*? As he was thinking, he began to write down a few questions: (1) Do you need to make a home visit or will a picture of the inside of the foster home be acceptable? (2) How long will the animals that are being fostered in my care remain with me?"

He made a call to the Riverview Shelter and decided to ask them his questions.

"Hello. Riverview Animal Shelter" was the response when the phone was answered.

Psych said, "I have a few questions about becoming a foster family for your shelter."

He was encouraged to ask his questions, so he began, "Do you always make a home visit or will pictures of the foster site be acceptable? How long will the animal fostered need to be in my care?"

The response to his first question was, "Pictures would be acceptable."

However, the second question required an explanation. "I'm unable to give you an exact length of time that you would foster an animal. It would depend on someone's request for adopting your fostered animal."

"How does that work?" Psych asked.

"You would be called and asked to bring the animal back to the shelter. Then the interested party would meet with the animal."

Understanding Sassie II

"Thank you," Psych said as he hung up the phone. *I believe I will soon go over to the shelter and see about fostering an animal or two.*

During the week, Ruth and Donald kept busy with the flow of Gulf Coast animal evacuations. Jim kept his promise, and his jet traveled non-stop from the Gulf Coast to Riverview and non-stop from Riverview to the Gulf Coast. Jim made sure that he had enough pilots to rotate their schedules to fly. He was pleased to help a good cause.

Psych went to the Riverview Shelter and filled out a Foster Home application. He attached the phony pictures of his site.

Jane took the time to review his application. Just as Psych had hoped, Jane was so very busy that she immediately agreed to have him take some of the Gulf Coast dogs home with him.

He selected two small mixed-breeds that seemed to be high-energy dogs. As he placed them into the car crates, he smiled and thought, *Success at last! Now I can work my dogs and schedule another big fight!*

Donald had been doing a good job with his recording of the Gulf Coast animal evacuation data. Because he had already created a computer database to record the Riverview Shelter animals' information, he felt that he could also use this computer spreadsheet for recording the Gulf Coast evacuation rescues. He just needed to add a few additional categories to his spreadsheets. This program had

77

already been helpful in doing a quick search or when a special mailing had been needed.

Donald was proud of the fact that he was able to record all the information on each evacuation animal within one hour of the animal's arrival at the Riverview Shelter. He even had a category for foster locations as well as those animals that had already been adopted from the Riverview Animal Shelter locations.

Mike had discovered that some of the foster locations had not been visited by a person from the Riverview Shelter. He asked Donald to print out the list of foster locations used by the Riverview Shelter for the Gulf Coast evacuation animals.

Donald handed the print-out list to Mike. When Mike looked over the list, he responded, "I recognize most of the foster homes on this list. They are kind-hearted people and give a lot of compassionate care. There is one foster name that I do not recognize. May I see the original file record?"

Mike began to study the file. He looked at the enclosed pictures showing the interior of the foster home. There was no report of anyone's making a visit to this home. That was when he looked at the physical address.

"This address can't be right!"

Donald reached for the application, and when he saw the physical address, he agreed, "THIS cannot be correct. I guess I made a major mistake in not listing the physical address into the computer. I just thought that because we had the GPS location, we did not need the physical address typed in. THIS address is the location of the County Maintenance Building!

"There is a phone number listed in their application," Donald added, "I think we should try to call this phone number."

Mike dialed the phone number; he heard a recording, "This phone is no longer in service."

As Mike hung up the phone, he told Donald, "I don't like this. Let's check the GPS location on these dogs!"

Using the GPS application on his computer, Donald was able to pinpoint the location of these dogs. He showed Mike the GPS location on the area map, "That's near the county line!"

Mike replied "I've never had to go out that far. I think I should give that county sheriff a call."

Mike dialed the number to that county's sheriff, and he took another look at the application. From that sheriff he learned that the nearby county's sheriff also seldom traveled to that GPS area.

Mike explained the reason for his call. "I'm concerned about the false information put on the foster care application. I want to make a visit to the area and see for myself if such a foster animal location exists. Would you like to join me?

The sheriff agreed to participate in this investigation and suggested that it might be wise for them to approach the location in the early morning. "I'll bring my two deputies. Let's plan to meet at the covered bridge on Route 714 at 6 a.m. tomorrow morning. I can show you a good shortcut to that GPS location," he added before he hung up.

16

PSYCH'S DOG FOSTER HOME

When Psych arrived home from the Riverview Shelter, he decided to place the caged foster dogs into a separate section of the barn. He did not want to place them near the area with his other dogs. *Even if they do howl or bark, no one will hear their voices in this sound-proofed barn*, he thought.

Psych was pleased and excited to know that another dog-fight plan would become a money-making reality very soon. He was thinking, tomorrow I'll introduce one of the foster dogs to Champ, and this should get Champ good and ready for the big fight.

His plan was to notify his dog-fight clients of the date of the next big fight and give the specific directions to his location. *I won't uncover the large red boulder until the day of the fight.* He had kept this marker covered with some hay and dirt. This way he could keep the location of the dog fight secret and difficult to locate until he wanted his clients to attend his night-time dog-fight.

Confident, he decided to celebrate his money-making expectations: a *whiskey toast to me for my brilliant ideas*. One drink led to another, and as the liquid soothed his palate, he soon fell into a comatose, drunken sleep.

At daybreak the next day, Mike and the nearby sheriff's team arrived at the covered bridge. Mike began to follow the county sheriff 's shortcut to the GPS location. The GPS led them around a run-down house to a hidden barn. Mike mused, *I'm glad we had a GPS to follow, or I never would have realized that there was a barn behind this house.*

In the house, Psych was still sound asleep. The dogs had heard the visitors, but their barking had not been heard outside the soundproofed barn.

The red boulder that was used as a marker for the dog-fight travelers was still covered with hay. It would only be uncovered just before a scheduled dog fight. Psych felt no need to post a guard because he had hidden the direction signs.

After the barn door had been kicked in, Mike's team quickly captured and sedated the dogs. As they looked around the barn, they began to realize what they were seeing.

The dogs that Psych had obtained as his foster animals were huddled in a corner of their crate.

"The foster dogs look like they are in good

shape," Mike said. "I believe we may have found these dogs just in time."

There was the evidence of blood all around the barn. Numerous crates lined the walls. Most of the crates were empty, but all the crates contained some blood spatter. There was a good-sized pit in the middle of the room, the location of the dog-fights.

Mike turned away from the scene, running off. He couldn't wait to escape this environment.

As the team entered the house, they found Psych asleep at the kitchen table. The empty whiskey bottle was on its side; the house smelled of dirty dishes and alcohol.

Psych's luck had run out. He was going to be rudely awakened and escorted to the County jail, the fate of Psych's dogs and property to be determined by the County judge.

17

RUTH'S AND JIM'S SATURDAYS

Saturdays were filled with Sassie's Read to Your Dog program at the library and her play time with Sharon. Jim suggested that Ruth and Sassie come to his home for an end-of-the-day meal. Jim loved to cook and wanted to show off his culinary skills to Ruth. Ruth did enjoy having a meal prepared for her. She did most of the cooking at the farm.

After dinner, Sharon would put on her pajamas and hop into bed. Sassie would cuddle with Sharon as she read a story to Sassie. They usually fell asleep together.

Ruth would help Jim clear the table and put the dishes into the dishwasher.

Jim began to explain their normal Sharon-and-father routine to Ruth. "Sharon and I usual play Scrabble for an hour every Saturday. Today she wanted to read to Sassie. Have you ever played Scrabble?"

Understanding Sassie II

Ruth laughed and replied, "I was the Scrabble champ for the county five years running. Let's see if you can beat me at that game. Let's play for one hour; the one with the highest number of points at the end of the hour will buy coffee for us the next time we meet!"

"It's a deal," Jim remarked. "I'll go get the game."

On his return to the kitchen, Jim peered into Sharon's bedroom; he saw Sharon reading to Sassie. He shared this bit of news with Ruth when he came with the game set.

With Jim's official Scrabble dictionary and Ruth's knowledge of competition rules, the game was both challenging and fun. Jim would make up silly words and Ruth would challenge them. "There is no such word as 'nottru,'" she said as Jim placed the letters on a double-word-score area.

"Yes, there is," he replied. "Haven't you heard someone say, 'not true'?"

Ruth laughed and responded, "Show me if this spelling is in the official dictionary!"

Jim never found his silly words in the dictionary, but he had fun teasing Ruth.

Jim always had a homemade batch of peanut butter-chocolate chip cookies that he'd serve for their snack.

As Ruth reached for another cookie snack, she said, "How am I going to stay slim and trim with all the delicious food you create? "

Jim's reply got to be their "running joke."

"No problem," he'd say. "We'll just schedule a 5k jog one of these weekends."

Ruth would laugh and reply, "With my busy schedule, it will be almost as much of a challenge to schedule that as refusing your tempting food."

They'd continue to laugh and talk as they played their Scrabble match.

At the end of the hour, they'd go into Sharon's bedroom where they would unfailingly find Sharon and Sassie fast asleep.

Ruth would whisper Sassie's name. When Sassie gently got off the bed, Ruth would hook the clip of the leash to her collar. With a whispered "good night" to Jim, Ruth and Sassie would go out to their car and head for home.

Ruth looked forward to this Saturday routine. She was beginning to enjoy Jim's company and wondered: *Am I starting to have special feelings about Jim*?

It was just before the Summer Break of school that Ruth scheduled a week-long-prep class for her CPDT test.

Jane reminded her to save her receipts for the scholarship re-imbursement.

18

RUTH, MILLIE, AND PUPPY SOCIALIZATION CLASS

The evacuations from the Gulf Coast animal shelters had been successful. Now the Gulf Coast was in the middle of clean-up, and in some areas, it was a job of rebuilding. The Riverview Animal Shelter was beginning to return to their normal routines.

Ruth and Millie had postponed their puppy class plans during this evacuation time but now felt they wanted to begin their educational and socialization curriculum.

"I think we should define the word 'socialization' and give a print-out of this definition to each person when they register," Millie said. "We want them to understand that socialization is the most important skill we can teach in the early life of a puppy.

"Positive socialization will help a puppy to be comfortable with a variety of places and people as well with as sounds and situations. "

Ruth agreed with that thought and added, "I believe we need to emphasize that all experiences during socialization should be happy, fun, and positive for the puppy."

Millie suggested, "I'd like to make this class a 'drop-in' class, because the first fifteen weeks in a puppy's life is the best time for good socialization, and I'd like to have as many opportunities for each team to have a chance to practice and learn about socialization skills."

"I agree," Ruth said. "I think we could use a clipboard method for teaching this class. Each page would have a different skill listed. Then we could put some of the various teaching examples that we may want to teach in class on each topic sheet."

"I like the idea," Millie responded. She then added, "We could check off and date the examples that we use in each class."

"Let's also include a 'tip of the day' page that would give each team a helpful suggestion," Ruth added. "I'm thinking about the hand-in-the-bowl method I use. I'd like the puppies always to think that something extra good will be given to them when a hand goes toward a puppy's bowl."

"I think we're ready to advertise," Millie concluded.

"Almost," Ruth said. "I'd like to have a veterinarian's letter of approval for a puppy to be able to take the class and a method of 'aging out' or 'graduation' to a Basic Manners Class."

Understanding Sassie II

Millie thought for a minute and agreed to the wisdom of what Ruth had said, "Let's go with a pre-registration, and we can give them a packet with rules and expectations at that time."

That made sense to Ruth. "Now, we can advertise."

19

MIKE AND MILLIE

Mike and Millie were taking Goldie for a walk. As they walked, Millie began to share her joys and concerns about the puppies that had been seized from the dog-fighter's farm.

"Some of those puppies that were seized may be a challenge to socialize," Millie was telling Mike.

Mike asked Millie, "Do you think the dog Psych named 'Champ' can be re-habilitated?"

"We've been giving him some natural relaxation remedies, and I've been playing some soothing music. This helps to calm him. I believe he is beginning to respond to my kindness, but it may take a long time for him to be able to be adopted."

Millie continued, "I'm not sure, but I do know that if he is ever adopted, it will need to be someone that will be patient with him and understand the dog's body language. I know one thing for sure.

He must always have a halter. He gets very agitated with a regular snap collar."

"I understand you are experimenting with a new private class, 'Solving Rover's Problems.'" Mike continued with a question, "Will that kind of a class help Champ?"

"Yes," Millie answered. "Eventually if we find the right forever-home, I believe that love will be stronger than the fear he has endured. Why would anyone treat a dog with the cruelty that Champ experienced?"

Mike shrugged his shoulders. He had no answer to Millie's question.

"I'm glad they have placed Psych's animals at the Riverview Animal Shelter," Mike responded. "I do believe that if they can have a chance at a normal life, you will be the one who can help them."

Millie started to disagree with his statement, "Actually, Ruth is doing most of the work on a puppy socialization class. I will be helping her with the class, but she really understands the value of positive dog training and knows what's best for the puppies in this class. She said that because the puppies are only 9 weeks old, we will still have a chance to modify any negative behaviors they have been learning.

"We plan to start the socialization classes the Monday after Ruth comes back from her class. We'll have some teenage volunteers that will help us work with these puppies."

Mike was thinking out loud when he said, "I'm

so thankful that I decided to place a GPS chip into all the Gulf-Coast-evacuated animals. We were able to rescue the two dogs that were fraudulently taken into foster care. Thankfully, these two dogs were not hurt."

Mike wanted to encourage Millie to tell him more about the socialization class, "I believe you said that you'd like to meet twice a week and have a constant enrollment. How are you planning to accomplish all you need to do in each class?"

Millie smiled. "Ruth is the smart one. She suggested a clipboard method for games to be played. She also felt it would be wise to have a veterinarian's written recommendation as a prerequisite for enrollment into the program.

"We'll be giving a packet of information when they enroll. There will be a copy of a report given by the Veterinarian's Association. It will explain the value of socialization during the 9-to-14-week period."

"Wow," Mike said, "I'm impressed! It sounds like you and Ruth are going to have an awesome class! I believe that when Ruth returns from her CPDT prepclass there will be a lot of fun for puppies as well as for humans."

20

RUTH AND HER CPDT TEST PREPARATIONS

Jane had been reading Ruth's CPDT-test-preparation-class report, when Ruth walked into her office.

"I've got a check for you. It's for your class-bill receipts. I was just reading your report, and I'm finding it interesting," Jane told Ruth.

She continued, "It looks like the instructor at this academy covered a lot of information and topics during your week-long stay there!"

Ruth nodded her head and said, "If you were to read the official test requirements, it states that, '(CPDT) measures a broad range of knowledge and skills in ethology, learning theory, dog training technique, and instruction.'"

She continued, "I believe this class covered all these topics and more. We even had our own shelter dog to train during that week. However, I will still need to have a signed attestation statement from a veterinarian, show that I have had at least 300 hours' experience in doing training within the last 3 years, sign a Standards of Practice and Code of Ethics form, as well as a Less Intrusive Minimally Aversive (LIMA) Effective Behavior Intervention form.

"Once this is completed, I will also need to send that paperwork and a non-refundable check to the Certification Council for Professional Dog Trainers. They will check over my paperwork and if it is acceptable, I will receive an entrance certificate with a place, date and time for the CPDT exam. I will need this certificate in order to be admitted for the exam."

"Wow!" Jane said. "There is a lot to do and know even before you take the exam!"

"Yes, and the check is non-refundable even if I do not pass the test. I would need to re-apply to retake the exam, with an additional fee, every time I wish to retake this exam."

"I'll write the check for your application. I know that you will pass it with no problems."

Ruth appreciated Jane's confidence in her. "I took a lot of notes and was able to keep all the tests that I took at the academy. My brain is so full it almost hurts. I can't wait to talk to Millie about this experience."

"Did someone say my name?" Millie asked as she walked into Jane's office.

Ruth gave Millie a hug, announcing, "I 've missed

Understanding Sassie II

you! I have a bunch of things that I've learned that I want to share with you!"

As the girls began to talk, Jane laughed and went back to reading Ruth's report.

21

PLANNING SOMETHING SPECIAL

When Jim heard that Ruth had returned from her CPDT prep-class, he called her. "Can we meet at the Riverview Park this afternoon and talk? I want to do something special for Sharon to celebrate her good grades and the hard work she has done all through this school year. School will be ending soon. I wanted to share my thoughts with you, but I don't want Sharon to hear about my plans as I'd like this to be a surprise."

Ruth and Jim had taken a seat overlooking the garden in the park, when Jim began to tell Ruth of his surprising-Sharon ideas. "I'd like to do something for Sharon that Sassie can attend," Jim began.

Ruth nodded yes. "Jim, Sassie served as a diabetic Service Dog for my mom. Sassie still has her Service Dog vest. Service Dogs, by law, may go anywhere with the human they are working with. Although Sassie is no longer working with my mom,

I believe she would have permission to enter with us at any location, especially if I asked the manager of the establishment ahead of time."

"That's great!" Jim said. "Sharon loves to play miniature golf. There is a huge indoor Mini-golf Fun Spot located just near the Riverview Mall. It is Sharon's favorite place. Maybe we could plan to surprise her with a visit to this location."

Then Jim realized how much Sassie loved to chase a ball and asked, "Would Sassie chase their golf balls?"

"Sassie knows she is working when she wears her vest and will not play during that time," Ruth explained. "I will check with the manager of that mini-golf park to be sure that Sassie would be allowed to attend. Let me know the date that we are we planning to go there."

Ruth suddenly remembered the Puppy Socialization class, "Oh, I almost forgot to ask about your plans for Monday night," and without giving Jim a chance to answer, she continued, "Monday at 6 p.m., we are going to have our first puppy socialization class. Would you and Sharon like to come and watch? Sassie will not be there, and Sharon would not be able to participate, but I believe both of you would enjoy seeing the puppies."

Jim smiled and replied, "I believe it would be a good experience for Sharon. She will be disappointed that Sassie will not be there, but yes, please plan on seeing us there."

The day of the miniature golf outing, there was an unexpected incident. It involved Sharon and Sassie, and it scared both Ruth and Jim. It proved that Sassie was not just a Therapy Dog but that she was still a Service Dog.

22

PUPPY SOCIALIZATION CLASS

The Large Group Instruction Room had a group of chairs arranged in a semi-circle. Each team (puppy and handler) had been encouraged to bring a small blanket or large towel for the puppy. This would be placed next to their chair.

The instruction sheet given at registration listed several examples of "high-value treats." Many of these high-value treats (cut into small pieces) were also expected to be brought for the class.

"Good evening, class," Millie began. "Welcome to a number of fun experiences and lots of laughter in this class. My name is Millie, and this is my co-instructor for the class, Ruth.

"We will take turns teaching and helping you practice a number of socialization skills. Many tips and suggestions will also be given to you for positive training. We believe in training with tools of love and building respect between you and your puppy.

"At the end of class, be sure to pick up your handout. This will review today's activities as well as have a schedule of the dates and times we will be offering socialization classes. You may attend as many as you wish of these classes. Just a reminder that after your puppy is 14 weeks old, you will be graduated to the Basic Class schedule.

"Now let's let the fun begin," Millie concluded and turned the class's attention to Ruth.

Ruth began her directions, "Instructions will be explained. Please listen to the complete instructions. You will have an opportunity to ask questions before we begin to follow these directions. We will be moving around the room and helping everyone as needed.

"When I say to do so, you will stand and pick up your puppy. Give your puppy a treat. Then hand the puppy to the person on your right. Take your time. When you receive the new puppy, smile and give a treat. If you wish to sit, you may, but if you do so, remember you will later need to get up to return the puppy to his human.

"Let's begin. Please stand and pick up your puppy. Give a treat. When ready, give your puppy to the human on your right. Remember to give the new puppy a treat and smile. I will pause for a minute as you enjoy this new bundle of fur.

"Now, return the puppy to his human. Give your puppy a treat and tell him what a good boy he has been. Place him on his blanket." Ruth concluded with, "At this time, you can relax as the next exercise is explained."

Millie began the next exercise by handing out a large T-shirt to every team. "I call this next game the 'Dress Your Puppy' game.

"Remember to wait until I say 'begin' before you dress your puppy.

"Once again, you will give your puppy a treat before you begin this exercise.

"Usually the best way to put on the T-shirt is to place the puppy's head into the shirt first. The front legs will be entered next.

"Give treats and praise all during the time you are dressing or undressing your puppy."

Ruth then said, "Please begin," as she started to move around the room. She repeated the instructions that Millie had given for the Dress Your Puppy exercise.

The games and fun continued.

They played a "Recall Game" and a "Climb a Step Game." They had the puppies walk on a rug and then on sand. There was the "Clicker/Noise Game" and a "Dark Glasses and Hat Game."

The Tip of the Day was the Food Dish Tip that Ruth explained, "You may use an empty bowl or even practice this while he is eating his supper. The key is to make sure you have a very high-value treat to put into the puppy's dish. I use a small bit of raw beef or chicken skin but remember that whatever you use, it must be rewarding to your puppy. Place the dish on the floor, and as the dog checks out the dish, let him know that you have a special treat for him. Slowly add the treat to the bowl. This can be done at every meal so that he knows that your hand means something good will happen.

"I'll pass out some empty bowls, and you can start with adding the treat you have to the dish. We will ask you to wait until one of us is beside you before you begin."

Ruth and Millie circled the room; they were pleased to see the results.

"Don't forget your hand-outs, and please have a safe trip home," Millie announced as she dismissed the class.

Sharon ran up to Ruth and hugged her. "That was awesome!" she announced. "I'm so glad we came. You are an awesome teacher!"

Ruth laughed and asked, "What about Miss Millie's teaching?"

"Oh, yes, she's okay, but you are the best!"

Jim announced, "Let's go, Sharon. You still have school tomorrow."

Sharon was still dancing around Ruth. She replied to her father, "Yes, but in only one week I'll be on summer break!"

She gave another hug to Ruth and skipped out the door.

Jim gave a quick wave to Ruth and followed his daughter to the car.

23

MINIATURE GOLF

The special day for Sharon arrived. Ruth had talked with the manager of the park, and he had agreed to let Sassie attend if she wore her Service Dog vest. When Sharon was told about her surprise, her first question had been, "Will Sassie be coming with us?"

Sassie wore her Service Dog vest, and everyone was smiling as they entered the miniature golf park.

That day Sharon had been drinking a large amount of soda. The day was hot, so no one took notice of Sharon's unusual consumption.

Sharon was excited to be able to play miniature golf with her best friend, Sassie. They began the series of challenges with smiles and anticipation of fun.

Sassie was staying particularly close to Sharon, but no one saw anything unusual with Sassie's close attention to her. Sassie was almost too close to her.

"Watch out, Sassie, I don't want to hit you with my golf club," Sharon repeatedly warned.

Arriving at the next miniature golf station, Sharon announced that she was tired, and she sat on a nearby bench.

It was there that Sassie did something she had not done in a long time. She jumped on Sharon.

Seeing Sassie do this, Jim said, "What the...?"

Ruth recognized the alert and after yelling, "NO!" she told Jim to call 9-1-1 for help. Ruth knew that Sassie was indicating Sharon was going into diabetic shock.

They saw Sharon begin to fall off the bench. Ruth knew that this was not the result of Sassie's alert, but a situation of danger.

The paramedics arrived almost immediately, and at Ruth's insistence. they tested Sharon's blood sugar.

"We need to get her to the hospital NOW!" they said when they saw her blood sugar results.

At the Emergency Room, the doctor informed Jim, "The paramedics got her here just in time. She was going into a diabetic shock. We've been able to lower her blood sugar level, but I would recommend that we keep her hospitalized for a few days and continue to regulate her sugar levels. I believe this dog may have saved your daughter's life."

Ruth wrapped her arms around Jim. She was thankful for Sassie's ability to sense the dangerous blood sugar levels in the human body, but she never thought that this ability would save Sharon's life.

Understanding Sassie II

"Jim," Ruth suggested, "let's go and have a cup of coffee at the hospital's cafeteria. The doctor wants Sharon to rest, and we need to take Sassie out of this area."

Jim looked at his daughter and saw that she was resting peacefully. "I think that may be a good idea."

The coffee was strong and hot. Jim was still in shock. *I almost lost my daughter!* he thought.

Ruth seemed to understand what Jim was thinking. She began to reassure him that his little girl was all right.

"What now?" Jim asked.

Ruth hated to see Jim so worried. She explained her mom's diabetic experience and added, "Diabetes can be controlled. The doctors will regulate her blood sugar and teach both her and you how to manage the blood sugar regulation on your own."

Ruth continued, "You will need to remember that she can live a long life if she follows the doctor's orders."

With a sigh of relief and with tears in his eyes, Jim said, "Ruth, you are a wise and very special person. How did I ever earn your care and compassion?"

Ruth had a lump in her throat; she had fallen in love with Jim. She wondered, as she hugged him, *does he feel the same about me?*

24

RUTH'S ACCIDENT

Sharon was being discharged from the hospital. Ruth had gone to Jim's home to help him get the house ready for Sharon's return.

"I'm glad you brought Sassie with you today. Sharon will be so happy to see her," Jim said.

He was getting ready to go out the door, but he decided it might be wise to ask Ruth to keep an eye on the roast in the oven. Jim had prepared a vegetable casserole and a pork roast for the night's dinner. "Ruth, please be sure to take out the roast at 3:00 p.m. I do expect to be home before that time, but if I am delayed, I'll need you to be sure it is out of the oven no later than 3. Otherwise, it will be overcooked and dry."

As she watched Jim drive away, she thought about Sassie and how she was once again a Diabetic Service dog. *I'm glad that Sassie has her old job back*, Ruth thought. Yet she had to admit that she was a

Understanding Sassie II

little jealous of the bond that Sharon and Sassie had developed.

She looked around the house and concluded it was almost ready for Sharon's arrival. *Maybe I should do a quick vacuum before they come home*, she thought.

Ruth pulled out the vacuum cleaner and during her quick run through the house, she became lost in her thoughts about Jim.

I think I am in love with him. Does he feel the same about me? What would it be like to be Sharon's stepmom? Is it too soon for him to think about getting married again? Her thoughts were a jumble of questions...with lots of mixed feelings.

Sharon was dressed and ready to go when her father arrived at the hospital. "The nurse said she needs to talk to you before we can go home," she told her father.

"I will have to go over the discharge instructions before you go home," the nurse explained. As she handed the sheets to Sharon's father, she made clear each of the directions and expectations, and after each section she would ask, "Do you understand this information?"

Jim and Sharon continued to nod their heads yes, and when the nurse was done with the directions, she called for a wheelchair.

"I'm okay to walk," Sharon announced.

"I realize that is true," the nurse replied, "but the

hospital policy is that you be wheeled in a wheel-chair to the vehicle that will be taking you home."

When Jim mentioned that he had made her favorite vegetable casserole and a roast for dinner, Sharon said, "I am hungry." But then he added the fact that Sassie was at the house waiting for her, and Sharon hopped into the wheelchair and said, "What are we waiting for? Let's go!"

Ruth finally finished her vacuuming, then glanced at the clock.

"Oh, NO!" she cried. "It is after 3:00 p.m.! I've got to get that roast out of the oven NOW!"

She started to hurry, and she forgot to watch where she was stepping. She tripped on the vacuum cleaner's electric cord. Falling, she grabbed for anything that might prevent the fall.

She bumped the end of the coffee table. Her momentum caused her to knock over a floor lamp and become entangled with that cord. When she finally landed, her arm hit something hard and she heard a loud snap.

That was when Sharon and Jim walked into the house. They discovered Sassie licking Ruth's face.

"You've got to get the roast out of the oven NOW!" Ruth announced.

Jim took one look at Ruth and called 9-1-1. "Don't move!" Jim ordered Ruth. He added, "Don't worry about the oven! I've called for an ambulance and they are on their way."

Jim did not touch Ruth. He feared doing anything

Understanding Sassie II

that might harm her or cause her more pain. He was frustrated but continued to talk quietly. Meanwhile, Sassie kept trying to kiss her face.

The ambulance soon arrived, and it transported Ruth to the Riverview Hospital in record time. Her arm was x-rayed. Indeed, it had been broken. "A clean break," the doctor said and added, "the ankle is badly sprained, too, but I will wrap it, and that should make it feel better."

"You are grounded, young lady!" Jim said to Ruth. "I want you to plan to stay at my home, and Sharon and I will be taking care of you. No arguments! I believe this is the best solution. I would never forgive myself if I let you go home to try to manage to care for yourself."

Ruth did like the idea of being cared for, but she also was afraid of becoming bored and restless. However, she began to realize how little she would be able to accomplish with her injuries.

Staying with them, she quickly came to enjoy Jim's cooking, and she loved to watch Sharon brush Sassie's hair and provide other loving actions. Sharon did a good job of changing the dog's water often and spoiled Sassie with long walks.

The most wonderful parts of being here, Ruth thought, *have been my long conversations with Jim.*

25

A TEDDY BEAR IN CLASS

Millie had heard the news about Ruth's accident. "What am I going to do with the upcoming Puppy Socialization Class without Ruth?" she asked Mike.

"Is there anything I can do to help?" he replied. "I'm not a dog trainer, but maybe I can somehow help with a part of the socialization."

"I have an idea," Millie said. "Do you remember that old Teddy bear costume that you wore on Halloween two years ago?"

"Yes, I believe it is stored in the attic."

"Do you know if it still fits you?" When Mike told her that he was sure it would still fit, Millie asked him to bring the outfit down from storage.

She explained her plan and added that Mike could help with a new socialization scenario. Mike liked the idea. He thought it would be fun.

Millie told Jane what she had planned to do for

the next Puppy Socialization Class, and Jane, too, said that it sounded like fun.

"Can I help?" Jane asked Millie.

"I was hoping you would," Millie replied. "I can really use an extra pair of hands and eyes."

The Puppy Socialization Class began; Millie introduced Jane and mentioned Ruth's accident. She continued, "I'd like to begin this week with a report from each team. How much socialization were you able to accomplish this week, and in what way was the socialization positive for your puppy? We'll begin with the first person on the right of the semi-circle."

After each team gave their report, Mille made a point of complimenting them.

"Just a reminder," Millie urged, "please be giving a treat to your puppy as a reward. In addition, use your happy voice to praise and encourage good behavior.

"Once again, I will give all the instructions before you are required to do anything. Only after I am sure that all understand, will I direct you to begin the task.

"Our first task will be an observation for your dog. We will have a visitor step into the doorway of this room. Your dog will no doubt notice this visitor. Reward quiet behavior. You may give a 'sit' request or even a 'down' if you wish. Ignore any barking. No rewards should be given for barking. When all the dogs are quiet, the visitor will leave. At this point you will give lots of praise and treats. I will now ask our visitor to come into the doorway."

Mike, dressed in his Teddy bear costume, appeared in the doorway. He said nothing but just stood there. Some of the dogs barked, but most of them quickly settled down.

Once the dogs were quiet, Mike disappeared.

"The Teddy bear will reappear, and we will repeat the first sequence. Remember to reward the dog when he is quiet and shows any type of willingness to settle.

"Come in again, visitor, please."

The Teddy bear returned to the doorway and this time the dogs settled quickly. When he left, the dogs were once again rewarded.

"I'd like to get the dogs up and moving before we start the next step of this experience," Millie announced.

"I would like you to walk your dogs around the room in a clockwise circle. Please go two complete circles then return to your seats. Please begin now," Millie said.

There was a chair in the corner of the room and Millie explained that this time the Teddy bear would come into the room and sit in the chair. "Once the bear is seated, I will instruct you to make a smaller circle around the room, staying closer to your chairs and further away from where the bear is sitting.

"Will the visitor come in and sit in the chair

Understanding Sassie II

please? Now I want the teams to begin to circle the room. Treat and reward your puppy when he pays attention to you and ignores the bear. Keep circling until I tell you to return to your seats."

They circled three times before Millie said, "Please return to your seats. Reward your puppies and keep their attention on you as our visitor leaves the room."

The dog owners then reviewed a few of their games and picked up their hand-outs as they left.

"Remember to practice at every opportunity," Millie reminded them.

"That was fun," Jane told Millie. "Can I work with you again?"

"Of course. I was hoping you would like to continue to help me."

As the weeks turned into months, Ruth discovered that she was beginning to get homesick. Although she enjoyed her time at Jim and Sharon's home, she missed some of the comforts of her own home. *I had that special quiet-time and my long, relaxing bubble-bath-time,* she remembered.

Her brother Donald came to visit from time to time, and Jim continued to make the best meals. Ruth continued to enjoy watching Sharon and Sassie play, but she was starting to become restless.

Ruth had been getting physical therapy on her ankle, and Jim had continued to be there by her side. He enjoyed giving her encouragement and lots of emotional support.

113

Jim had discovered there was a strong, wise, and sensitive person inside this beautiful woman named Ruth.

I believe I have fallen in love with her, he thought.

26

RUTH GOES HOME

The orthopedic doctor was examining Ruth's injuries and said, "You probably would have been better off if you had broken this ankle."

Surprised by this statement, Ruth responded, "Why do you say that?"

"You have injured many of the muscles and tendons in your ankle. If you had broken the ankle, there would have been less damage to these areas, and this area would have healed a lot faster."

He continued, "I've checked the x-ray of your arm, and it looks like you have healed nicely. I think we will plan to remove the cast next week."

"Does that mean I can take a nice long, soaking bath?" Ruth asked in a hopeful voice.

"Yes, I believe that would be a good idea and certainly would help soothe your body. However, be careful NOT to reinjure your ankle. You have come a long way in the healing process, and it would be a major problem if you were to re-injure this ankle.

"Keep up with the physical therapy appointments. The therapists will continue to guide you. At this time, the crutches are now becoming a balancing support for you. Again, I want to remind you that you will need to keep using the crutches until you are instructed that the crutches are no longer needed.

"I understand there will be a temptation to walk on the ankle, but if you put too much weight on the injured ankle too soon, it will delay the full healing of this bad sprain."

As Jim was driving Ruth back to his home, he heard her say, "I want to go home next week. Once the cast is off, I'd really like to soak in my own bathtub."

"Oh," Jim replied, "I hope you realize that you are more than welcome to stay with us for a longer time."

The week passed too quickly for Jim and way too slowly for Ruth. She had packed the few things she had brought to Jim's house and was ready to leave an hour before the cast-removal appointment time.

"I just can't wait to get this itchy cast off my arm." She announced this to Jim as they began the short trip to the orthopedist's office.

When the cast was removed, Ruth was ready to dance with joy. Seeing her happiness and suspecting that she wanted to dance, the doctor quickly said, "No, don't even think about it!"

In the car ride to Ruth's home, Jim tried to tell Ruth about his feelings for her, "I have enjoyed your company greatly while you have stayed at my home...."

"Yes," Ruth said, "I am grateful for all the care and kindness you have given me and Sassie, and we have enjoyed your company."

Still nervous, but trying to propose to Ruth, he said, "Sharon has enjoyed playing with Sassie...."

Having reached Ruth's home, Jim carried Ruth's personal items into the house. He began to repeat more comments about Sharon and Sassie.

"It has been great to have the assurance that Sassie can alert us if Sharon has a diabetic problem. Sharon has the bonus of playing with Sassie."

Getting even more nervous, Jim continued, "it would be awesome for Sharon if you and I were to get married."

"What?" Ruth looked at Jim in surprise. "What are you saying? Are you only asking me to marry you so that Sassie could be with Sharon? How DARE you!"

Hurt and disappointed, Ruth asked Jim to leave.

Donald walked into the room just as Jim was leaving.

Seeing tears in Ruth's eyes, he gave his sister a hug and whispered, "I'm glad to have you home."

27

SASSIE CONCERNS

Donald traveled to Jim's house and brought Sassie home.

After Sassie came home, Ruth noticed that Sassie seemed to have little or no energy. Concerned, she also noticed that unlike Sassie's normal appetite, when she usually gobbled her food, she now would only pick at it. Also, Sassie no longer followed Ruth around, but was often found lying in her crate.

"I thought she would be happy to be home," Ruth told Donald. "She has not been interested in playing with any of her toys. She even refuses to play with her favorite ball. Do you think she is sick?"

As Donald looked at Sassie, he replied, "No, I don't think she is sick. She looks like she is sad. She did spend a lot of time playing with Sharon."

Sassie was unhappy. She wished that Ruth realized just how much she missed Sharon. *I had the*

Understanding Sassie II

perfect job again, Sassie thought, *I was once again a Diabetic Alert Service Dog. I even continued being a "Read to Your Dog" dog for Sharon.*

Sassie did have feelings. *I wish Ruth would realize that dogs do have feelings. I am very sad and depressed.*

Donald suspected that Ruth was sad, too. He wondered what had happened to Ruth and Jim's relationship. *They were so very happy whenever they were together.*

"Do you want to visit Sharon and Jim this weekend?" Donald asked. "I can drive you over to their home."

"Probably not," Ruth answered softly, sadly.

This surprised Donald. "Why not?"

"I do NOT want to talk about it!" Ruth responded in a voice that seemed to emphasize that the subject was NOT open for discussion.

Meanwhile, in her home, Sharon missed seeing Sassie: *we used to get together on Saturdays.*

"Isn't Ruth going to visit us anymore?" Sharon asked her father.

"I'm not sure," Jim admitted.

"Can we visit her, so I can play with Sassie?"

Jim was not sure this would be a good idea, but he said, "You can call Miss Ruth and talk with her. Maybe she would like your company."

"If she would like my company," Sharon asked her father, "would you come with me?"

Jim wanted to be honest with his daughter, but

he wasn't sure how much to tell about his proposal to Ruth.

"I think I need to explain about my conversation with Ruth last week," he began to tell Sharon about his botched marriage proposal.

28

SHARON EXPLAINS

Ruth answered the phone on the second ring. "Hi, Miss Ruth," she heard Sharon say, "I miss seeing you!"

Ruth was surprised to hear Sharon's voice and at the same time, she felt guilty for not having given Sharon an opportunity to play with Sassie.

"Is everything all right?" Ruth asked, fearing Sharon had called because there was a problem with her father.

"Yes, all is okay. There's no problem here. I just wondered if I could come over and play with Sassie?"

"Sure! Come right on over. Will your Dad be coming?"

"No, he was called into work, but he said I could come visit Sassie, if I received permission from you."

An hour later, Sharon rang the doorbell. As Ruth opened the door and Sassie heard Sharon's voice,

Hurricane Sassie blew in and gave Sharon a shower of kisses.

"Sassie, let Sharon come into the house!" Ruth instructed her whirling dog.

Laughing, Sharon picked up Sassie's favorite ball, and the two moved outside to play in the fenced backyard.

After a couple of hours of playing, Sharon and Sassie came into the kitchen. Sassie went to her water bowl and began to drink.

Seeing this, Ruth asked, "Sharon, would you like a cold glass of lemonade?"

Sharon nodded her head yes and then remembered her manners. "Thank you. We both were thirsty."

"Can we talk?" Sharon asked, a bit shyly.

Ruth smiled and said, "Of course. What did you want to talk about?"

Sharon studied her glass of lemonade. She attempted to begin but then stopped. She was just not sure how to talk about her father's botched proposal.

"Do you realize how happy my dad has been whenever you are with him?"

Ruth was surprised at Sharon's words but also realized their truth. Jim seemed always to be laughing when they were together.

"What do you mean?" Ruth asked.

"I'm telling you that my father loves you! Right now, he is sad and miserable about his botched marriage proposal.

Understanding Sassie II

"When you were injured and living with us for those months, I realized that I had not seen Dad that happy since Mom died.

"Dad recently explained what he had said to you. It was a terrible proposal. He recognizes that now. He was just so nervous. He knew he was in love with you...and was not sure if you felt the same way about him.

"Please forgive his bad proposal and talk to him. You do love him, don't you?....and I really would love to have you become my mom."

Ruth's mouth dropped open as she began to realize that Sharon was saying the truth. "When will your dad be coming to get you?"

Sharon looked at the kitchen clock. "He should be coming in about an hour."

Ruth said, "That is plenty of time to order a pizza. Do you think he would be willing to have a pizza for dinner here instead of bringing you right home?"

"Pizza!" Sharon's eyes lit up as she squealed, "I'd love pizza for dinner!"

When Jim rang the doorbell, Sharon ran to the door and shouted to her father, "Say 'yes'! You must say 'yes!'"

"What are you so excited about?" Jim asked his daughter.

"Pizza for dinner. Miss Ruth invited us to have pizza for dinner. You MUST say 'YES!'"

Sassie had been nudging Sharon's elbow during the talk Sharon had been having with her father.

Feeling that her Dad fully realized that his daughter wanted them to stay for pizza, Sharon decided to leave the two adults alone together, and she skipped out the back door and began to play with Sassie.

"I guess we are staying for dinner," Jim said with a puzzled look on his face.

This left Ruth the job of explaining the pizza dinner offer and giving a major apology for her harsh reaction to Jim's awkward proposal of marriage.

"Jim, you have been so kind to me! I now realize that you did not understand that I have fallen in love with you. I wasn't sure if you felt that way about me. You never told me that you loved me, and when you said what you did about Sharon and Sassie, I felt you only wanted a marriage of convenience. I am so sorry! I should have known that the happiness we have shared has come from a genuine love."

Jim slowly smiled and responded, "Remember the day you said that you were sorry about the past? We were behind the library, and Sharon was playing with Sassie. Do you remember what I said to you on that day?"

"You told me that it's not a mistake if we learn from it," Ruth whispered.

"Well, I made a big mistake in asking you in a very clumsy way to marry me."

Getting down on one knee, he said, "Now, I would like to do this properly: Ruth, you are one very special woman, and I would be honored if you would agree to marry me and become my wife."

With tears in her eyes and happiness in her heart, she said the word Jim had long hoped to hear, "YES!"

CAST OF CHARACTERS

(in order of appearance)

Peg: Teenager; friend of Patrick

Lady: Goldie's puppy; Peg's dog

Patrick: Teenager; friend of Peg

Pal: Goldie's puppy; Patrick's dog

Millie*: Dog behaviorist; Mike's wife

Goldie*: Golden-Retriever-mix dog
Mike and Millie's dog
Mother of Sassie, Lady and Pal

Mike:* Animal Control Officer

George ("Psych"):	Runs a dog fighting business
Champ:	A prize dog-fighting dog
Jane*:	Supervisor of Riverview Animal Shelter
Ruth*:	volunteer at shelter;
Donald*:	Stepbrother to Ruth; volunteer at the shelter
Sassie*:	Goldie's puppy; Ruth's dog
Valerie*:	Ruth and Donald's mother
Pretty Girl:	Kitten adopted by Donald
Sharon:	Jim's young daughter
Jim*:	A corporate boss; once worked with Ruth

* Appeared previously, in *Understanding Sassie*.

GLOSSARY/VOCABULARY

Check-in: Dog decides to come back to person without being called

Electronic shock collar: A buckle collar that gives a painful shock

Lip flick: Tongue quickly licks the lips

Play bow: Dog leans forward with front elbows on the ground as hips stay in the air.

Service Dog: Dog that is, by law, required to accompany its human. The dog is needed for someone's life-function (example: Seeing-Eye dog)

Socialization: Important skills usually taught in the early life of a puppy. A positive variety of new experiences in areas such as people, places, sounds and situations

Therapy Dog: Dogs that give love and support. They are not covered by Service Dog laws

ABOUT THE AUTHOR

Helen Bemis has enjoyed working with dogs all her life.

She is grateful for the opportunity to help others understand these loving companions, as she endeavors to enrich the human-dog bond through tools of love.

She grew up on a dairy farm in Upper New York State; after graduating high school, she attended Albany Medical Center School of Nursing. She is married and has three children.

She has obtained a college degree at SUNY Adirondack, earned the Certified Professional Dog Trainer international certification and has a successful business, K-9 Karing. She has been a Therapy Dog evaluator and is an A. K. C. award evaluator. She has judged fun dog matches, often speaks to many organizations, and teaches dog safety and other dog-related topics to schools as well as at her local college.

She loves to hear people say, "Helen has gone to the dogs."

Contact Helen via:

K-9 Karing, LLC
Helen Bemis, CPDT-KA
P.O. Box 67
Ganesvoort, NY 12831-0067
Phone: 518.584.5357
Email: K9KaringHelen@ncap.rr.com

ABOUT THE ARTIST

MECHELLE ROSKIEWICZ
29 Fourth Avenue, Warrensburg, NY 12885
Cell phone: 518-744-7911
loveddogsart@gmail.com, loveddogsart.com

Creating animal-inspired art and one-of-a-kind portraits in painting and sculpture, artist Mechelle Roskiewicz captures their loving spirit and beauty. She has commissions throughout the United States and the world, including paintings in the Kennel Club of England's Library, CEO's Office and their prestigious Art Room in London. Published in magazines, books and producing illustrations, she continues to explore and expand her passion for art.

Mechelle lives in Warrensburg, NY, with her husband, James, and her two muses, Lilly and Ella, both Cavalier King Charles Spaniels.

REVIEW THIS BOOK?

Authors and their readers rely heavily on reviewers to help them find each other. Please help by writing a review wherever you wish.

Amazon.com sells more than half the books sold in the US; to review this book there, find *Understanding Sassie II* in their Books category and click on the button "Write a customer review." It will be appreciated.

CPSIA information can be obtained
at www.ICGtesting.com
Printed in the USA
BVHW041034230519
549124BV00014B/693/P